Industrial Studies

A workbook for building craft students

Peter Brett

Hammersmith and West London College

Stanley Thornes (Publishers) Ltd

Originally published in 1987 by Hutchinson Education
Reprinted 1988, 1989

Reprinted again in 1989 by
Stanley Thornes (Publishers) Ltd
Old Station Drive
Leckhampton
CHELTENHAM GL53 0DN
Reprinted 1990

British Library Cataloguing in Publication Data
Brett, Peter, 1950–
    Industrial studies: a workbook for
    building craft students.
    1. Building
    I. Title
    624   TH145

ISBN 0 7487 0267 9

Typeset in Times
Printed and bound in Great Britain by
Butler & Tanner Ltd, Frome and London

Contents

Preface

The aim of this book is to provide an information resource and student workbook for building-craft industrial studies. As such, it is equally suitable for either adoption as a main course text for use by all students to provide the basis of teaching and assessment material, or alternatively for use by the individual to reinforce, supplement or revise college lectures.

Industrial Studies is an integral component of all City and Guilds of London Institute Craft Certificate courses. The contents of this common component are the same for all students, irrespective of their chosen craft specialism. Its purpose is to equip students with a knowledge of the forms and elements of construction, the total building process, the structure of industry, and the relevance of the industry to society in general.

The course of study consists of three main areas:

1 Elements, functions and principles of construction

2 The process of building and the building team

3 Construction, the environment and the community

This workbook has been divided into three parts in accordance with these areas. The three parts are further subdivided into a number of separate topics. Each of these begins with a list of learning objectives and ends with an assignment to be completed after study. This will enable students to gauge their understanding and progress, and may also form the basis of coursework assessment. In addition, each separate topic ends with a series of multiple-choice or short-answer self-assessment questions.

This *Industrial Studies workbook* will undoubtedly be suitable for pupils involved in Technical and Vocational Educational Initiative (TVEI) Schemes, and for Certificate in Pre-Vocational Education (CPVE) students for the core as well as the construction specific exploratory and preparatory modules. It will also be useful for those studying for General Certificate in Secondary Education (GCSE) construction qualifications.

The author wishes to thank the following:

Cuprinol for photographs of timber decay and wood-boring insects.

Statutory forms are reproduced with the permission of The Controller of Her Majesty's Stationery Office, who reserve Crown Copyright.

Objectives are reproduced with the kind permission of The City and Guilds of London Institute.

Finally, I would like to dedicate this book to Harry who was always a constant source of inspiration and encouragement.

Introduction

The questions most frequently asked by building students and those considering a career in the industry are:

What is the scope of the building industry?
What can I become in the building industry?
What education/training will I receive?

Scope of the building industry

The 'building industry' in its widest sense covers *four* main areas of work:

Building
This is the construction, maintenance and adaption of buildings ranging from office blocks, industrial complexes and shopping centres to schools, hospitals, recreation centres and homes.

Civil engineering
This is the construction and maintenance of public works such as roads, railways, bridges, airports, docks and sewers etc.

Mechanical engineering
This is the installation, commissioning and maintenance of lifts, escalators and heating, ventilation, sprinkler and plumbing systems etc.

Electrical engineering
This is the installation, commissioning and maintenance of various electrical and electronic devices.

Within this complex structure there is a variety of specific job functions and careers, giving employment to about 1.2 million (approximately 6% of Britain's total workforce) plus about 325,000 self-employed. These are men and women working in offices and on sites all over Britain.

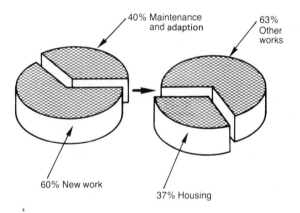

Figure 1   *Type of work*

The value of the work carried out annually by the industry is about £21,250 million (approximately 6% of Gross Domestic Product). This can be attributed as shown in Figure 1 to 60% new work and 40% maintenance and adaption. Of this total, about 37% is spent on housing and the remaining 63% is spent on other works.

Although a major employer, the industry is possibly one of the most disjointed. Of the total workforce, private contractors account for about

88% of those employed. The remaining 12% are employed by the direct-labour building departments of public authorities, a large proportion of whose work is concerned with maintenance and repairs. There are some 77,000 private contracting firms who employ two or more people. Whilst there are a number of very large contracting firms with several thousand employees, the vast majority (92%) employ less than 25 people.

Careers in the building industry

The building industry offers employment in *four* distinct career areas: professional; technician; building crafts; building operatives.

Professional
These graduate-entry positions include the following:

Architects
Who design and supervise the construction of buildings.

Engineers
These can be either civil engineers (concerned with roads and railways etc.), structural engineers (concerned with the structural aspects of a building's design) or service engineers who plan building-service systems.

Surveyors
These can also be either land surveyors (who determine positions for buildings, roads and bridges etc.), building surveyors (who are concerned with the administration of maintenance and adaption works as well as new buildings), quantity surveyors (who measure and describe building works using information contained on architects' drawings; in addition they also prepare valuations of works in progress).

Technician
This is the link level in the industry between the professional and craft areas. The main job functions of technicians are as follows:

Architectural technician
This involves the interpretation and presentation of the architect's design information, into a form suitable for use by the builder.

Building technician
Who is involved with the estimating purchasing, site surveying, site management and documentation of building works.

Building surveying technician
May specialize in building maintenance, building control or structural surveys etc.

Quantity surveying technician
Calculates costs and payments for building works.

Building crafts
The building crafts involve the skilled operatives who work with specific materials and actually construct the elements of a building. The main examples are as follows:

Bricklayer
Who works with bricks and mortar to construct all types of walling also concerned with maintenance and adaption of existing works.

Carpenter and joiner
They work with timber, other allied materials, metal/plastic items and ironmongery. They make, fix and repair all timber components in buildings.

Electrician
Works with metals, plastics, wire and cables, and installs and maintains electrical systems.

Formworker
Works with timber, metal and plastic etc. to produce a structure that supports and shapes wet concrete until it has become self-supporting.

Painter and decorator
They work with paint, paper, fabrics and fillers, to decorate or re-decorate new and existing

works; sometimes glaze windows and carry out sign writing.

Plasterer
Works with plaster, cement mixes, plasterboard and expanded metal, to finish walls ceilings and floors; also makes and fixes plaster decorations.

Plumber
Works with metals, plastics, and ceramics; installs tanks, baths, toilets, sinks, basins, rainwater goods, boilers, radiators, and gas appliances; also cuts and fixes sheet-metal roof covering and flashing and sometimes glazing; also maintains existing works.

Roof slater and tiler
Works with felt, timber, metals, mortar and a wide variety of slates and tiles. Covers new or existing pitched roofs with slates or tiles; also maintains existing works.

Shopfitter
Works with timber, metal, glass and plastics etc. Makes and installs shop fronts and interiors; also banks, hotels, offices and restaurants.

Stonemason
Works with stone and mortar. 'Bankers' cut and smooth stone while 'fixers' erect prepared stones.

Wall and floor tiler
Works with clay-ceramic/plastic tiles, adhesives and mortar; cuts and fixes floor and wall tiles; also mosaics.

Woodworking machinist
Operates a wide range of woodworking machines; prepares timber for the production of timber-building components.

Building operatives
There are *two* main types of building operatives employed on-site:

General building operative
Who uses various items of plant, e.g. hand tools, power tools, compressors and concreting equipment etc.; mixes concrete, mortar and plaster; lays drainage, kerb-stones and concrete etc.; off-loads materials and transports around site; also generally assists work of craft operatives.

Specialist building operative
Who carries out specialist building operations, e.g. ceiling fixer, dry liner, glazer, mastic asphalter, plant mechanic, roof sheeter and cladder, scaffolder, etc.

Building education/training schemes

The education/training scheme embarked upon will be dependent on the area of the industry wherein it is intended to gain employment. As this book is aimed at the building-craft operative, only this area of work is considered here.

There are *three* main methods of gaining entry into a building-crafts scheme:

1   Entry into a full-time Construction Industry Training Board (CITB) training programme, which consists of a block-release pattern of education/training at a college, together with practical-work experience with a building employer. Suitable persons may secure a two-and-a-half year apprenticeship. During the apprenticeship, release will be given to attend a block pattern of education/training at a college. Opportunities exist to gain the Craft and Advanced Craft Certificate of the City and Guilds of London Institute (CGLI) and Regional Examining Bodies.

2   Direct entry employment with a building employer. A three-year apprenticeship is required, during which release from work will be given to attend a part-time day or block pattern of education/training at a college. Opportunities to gain the Craft and Advanced Craft Certificate of the CGLI and Regional Examining Bodies are available.

3   Attendance on a one-year full-time college building-craft course; a non-CITB training

course or a CPVE course. On completion, suitable persons may be able to obtain a three-year apprenticeship with a building employer, during which release from work will be given to attend a part-time day or block pattern of education/training at a college. Opportunities to gain the Craft and Advanced Craft Certificate of the CGLI and Regional Examining Bodies are again available.

There are no formal qualifications for building-craft entry, although relevant G/CSEs will give a better chance of selection. Most people who apply for a CITB training programme will have to take their selection tests. Many colleges and other training schemes require a personal interview and or selection test before offering full-time course places.

In addition to the CGLI Certificates, during their apprenticeship period, most building-craft operatives will take a practical skills' test administered by the CITB. Successful completion of a skills' test coupled with a CGLI Craft Certificate will lead to a Certificate of Craft Recognition, awarded by the National Joint Council for the Building Industry (NJCBI).

On satisfactory completion of the apprenticeship period, there are many opportunities for suitable persons to enhance their future career prospects, by studying for further technical qualifications.

Part one

Elements, Functions and Principles of Construction

After working through this part of the book the student should be able to:

1 Recognize different forms of buildings and the main principles involved in their construction.

2 Recognize the main elements of a building.

3 Recognize the function and principles of each element.

4 List the main groups of building materials and their uses.

5 Sketch given elements and state the relative positions of components.

6 Recognize common faults, defects and failures in buildings.

Purpose and types of buildings

The majority of buildings and structures are constructed for a specific purpose. This will determine their shape, style, quality and therefore cost.

A building encloses space and in doing so creates an internal environment. The actual structure of a building is termed the *external envelope*. This protects the internal environment from the outside elements (known as the *external environment*). The protection role of this envelope is to provide the desired internal conditions for the building's occupants with regard to security, safety, privacy, warmth, light and ventilation. A structure can be defined as an organized combination of connected elements (parts), which are constructed to perform some required function, e.g. a bridge. The term *building* takes this idea a step further and is used to define structures that include an external envelope.

Many different types of construction are required to fulfil the needs and expectations of today's ever-demanding society. These consist of accommodation and facilities for living, working, recreation, religious activities, storage and transport. Collectively, these constructions are known as the *built environment*, whilst individually they are known as *elements* (parts) of the built environment (Figure 2).

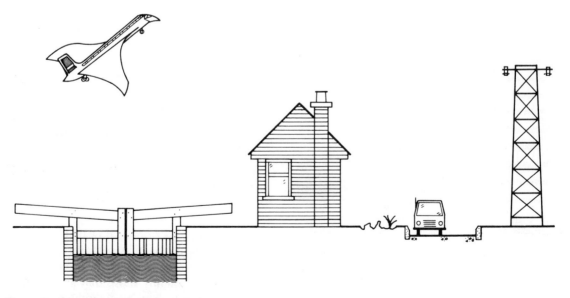

Figure 2 *Elements of the built environment*

Living accommodation

Units of living accommodation are termed *dwellings* (a place of residence or home). The purpose of a dwelling is to provide humans with a shelter from the external environment and a place of storage for their goods and chattels (all their movable property). A wide range of dwellings is required to suit the individual members of a society, e.g. ground-floor dwellings with easy access for the elderly or physically handicapped, small dwellings for single persons and couples, and a wide range of dwellings from small to large to suit various sized families. The quality, location and facilities offered by these various dwellings will also vary widely to suit current market/economic forces. Most new domestic-building work in the private sector is for purchase whilst that in the public sector is for renting.

Ideally, a dwelling should incorporate either a communal or private garden/open space to satisfy people's recreational needs, e.g. gardening, relaxing in the sun etc. Unfortunately, this facility is sometimes neglected: a factor which is often stated as one of the root causes of some present-day social problems (apathy, delinquency, frustration and vandalism). Dwellings may be divided into three building types according to their height as illustrated in Figure 3.

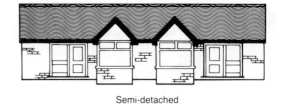
Semi-detached

Detached chalet

Figure 4   *Bungalows*

Low-rise buildings: from one to three storeys
Medium-rise buildings: from four to seven storeys
High-rise buildings: those above seven storeys

These categories can be further sub-divided in order to identify a wide variety of basic shapes, styles and groupings of dwellings.

Glossary of dwelling terms (see Figures 4 and 5)
Apartment   A set or suite of rooms that forms a complete dwelling.
Bungalow   A one-storey house.
Chalet   A small, light wooden-built dwelling. Bungalows with rooms in the wooden roof framing are known as *chalet bungalows*.
Cottage   A small house in the country. Originally intended for farm labourers. Hence terms such as cottage industry and cottage cheese etc.
Crescent   A terrace of dwellings in curved form.
Detached   A house or bungalow that is separate and unconnected from its adjacent ones. 'Link detached' is a term used by some building developers to signify those that are joined in some small way often by a garage or carport.

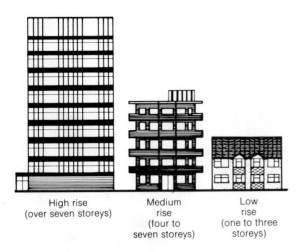

High rise (over seven storeys)   Medium rise (four to seven storeys)   Low rise (one to three storeys)

Figure 3   *Height of buildings*

Detached

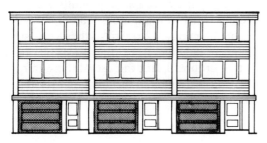

Terraced town houses

Figure 5 *Houses*

Flat A dwelling in a building of more than one storey. Accommodation usually in a block and being part of one storey forming a separate dwelling, access to which is via a communal entrance. See also *Apartment* and *Maisonette*. Flats may be 'purpose built' or conversions (created from existing large houses).

House A building of two or more storeys used for dwelling.

Maisonette A dwelling occupying part of a larger building, but unlike a flat has a separate outside entrance. May also be purpose built or a conversion.

Mews Traditionally, a street or a yard containing horse stables. Mainly now converted to form mews houses and mews apartments.

Penthouse A dwelling at the top of a block of flats which can be more than one storey. Often more lavishly equipped than the remainder of the block. Usually termed the Penthouse apartment or suite.

Semi-detached A house which is joined to one adjacent house, but detached from other buildings. Thus it shares a party wall (dividing wall).

Studio Traditionally, an artist workshop but now used for a one room apartment or flat.

Tenement. A block of apartments or flats, often with certain shared communal facilities. Mainly situated in the poorer inner-city areas.

Terrace A row of three or more houses, the inner ones of which share two-party dividing walls.

Townhouse Traditionally, a well-to-do person's house in the town owned in addition to their house in the country. Now taken to be any house over two storeys, often terraced.

Villa A detached or semi-detached suburban or country house.

Working accommodation

This can be divided into four main groups: industrial, shops, offices and educational. Once again, they can be described as being either low, medium or high rise.

Industrial Includes factories, workshops, mills, shipyards, steelworks and mineworks etc.

Shops A building where goods are sold including all places where an exchange of services takes place.

Offices Buildings used for the administration or clerical work in connection with a business or organization.

Educational Buildings used for all educational purposes, e.g. schools, colleges and universities.

Recreational accommodation

All buildings fulfilling a recreation role. This will include sports centres, swimming pools, stadiums, theatres, cinemas and concert halls in addition to art galleries, museums, libraries and any assembly/meeting hall.

Religious accommodation

Any building used as a place of worship to cater for a person's spiritual needs, e.g. church, temple, mosque or synagogue.

Storage accommodation

A building or space within a building used for storage or distribution of supplies, e.g. warehouse, gas silo, water-towers and reservoirs, petrol depots and oil tanks etc.

Facilities for transport

These include a wide range of routes, buildings and structures for road, rail, air and waterborne modes (canal, river and sea) of transport, e.g. roads, motorways, railways, runways, bridges, tunnels, viaducts, aquaducts, locks, docks, piers, flyovers and interchanges etc. In addition, this category also includes all allied buildings such as terminal complexes for bus, coach, rail, air and sea travel, motorway services' areas and associated storage buildings.

Purpose groups

Another method of categorizing buildings is by purpose groups, as shown in Table 1. Originally this method was introduced to group buildings according to their fire risk, e.g. multi-occupancy buildings which contain more than one dwelling present a greater fire risk than do single dwellings and therefore they are placed in separate groups. Later the use of these purpose groups was extended to include other regulatory functions.

Table 1 **Purpose groups**

Main category	Purpose group	Intended use
Residential	*Dwelling house* (not a flat or maisonette)	Private dwelling house
	Flat (including a maisonette)	Self-contained dwelling not being a house
	Institutional	Hospitals, schools and homes used as living accommodation for persons suffering from disabilities owing to illness, old age, physical or mental disorders and those under five years old, where these persons sleep on the premises
	Other residential	Residential accommodation not included in previous groups, e.g. hotels, boarding houses, and hostels, etc.
Non-residential	*Assembly*	Public building or assembly building where people meet for social, recreational, or business activities (not office, shop or industrial)
	Office	All premises used for administration procedures, e.g. clerical, drawing, publishing and banking etc.
	Shop	All premises used for the retail sale of goods or services, including restaurants, public houses, cafes, hairdressers and hire or repair outlets
	Industrial	All premises defined as a factory in Section 175 of the Factories Act (1961), not including slaughter houses etc.
	Other non-residential	All places used for the deposit or storage of goods, the parking of vehicles and other premises not covered in the previous non-residential groups

Self-assessment questions

Question   *Your answer*

1 Define the term 'the built environment'

_____

_____

_____

_____

2 List *four* main elements of the built environment

_____

_____

_____

_____

3 Name the term given to a curved terrace of houses

_____

_____

_____

_____

4 Sketch a chalet bungalow

5 Define the term 'external envelope'

_____

_____

_____

_____

6 List the requirements of the external envelope

_____

_____

_____

_____

7 Describe the main difference
  between a flat and a
  maisonette

  _____

  _____

  _____

  _____

8 State the term used to describe an eight-storey
  building

  _____

  _____

  _____

  _____

9 State the most suitable type
  of dwelling for an elderly
  couple

  _____

  _____

  _____

  _____

10 Name *two* types of storage
   accommodation

  _____

  _____

  _____

  _____

Structural forms

There are many differing structural forms in present-day use, each changing from time to time, in order to make the best possible use of new materials and developing techniques. These differing forms may be grouped together under three main categories: *Solid structures*; *framed structures*; and *surface structures*.

Solid structures

Also known as *masswall construction*. The walls of this type of construction combine the dual functions of supporting (load bearing) and protecting (external envelope). This form of construction is suitable for low- to medium-rise buildings where very large floor areas are not required. Solid construction normally takes the form of either brickwork, blockwork, stonework or mass concrete. It can be divided into two main types (cellular and crosswall) as illustrated in Figure 6.

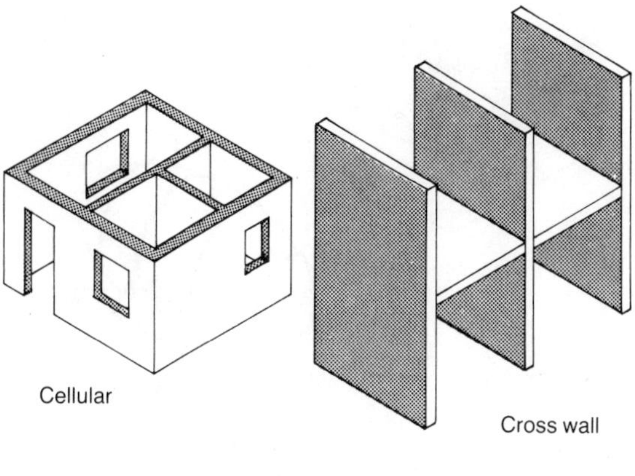

Cellular

This consists of an interconnected arrangement of internal and external walls, forming the cells (rooms) of the building. This results in a structure that is rigid, stable and load sharing.

Crosswall

This consists of a series of independent walls, built parallel to each other and at right angles to the front of the building, the front and back faces being infilled with non-load bearing external walls (curtain walls) having only a protecting function. As the free-standing cross-walls are inclined to be unstable, it is essential that the floors are rigidly tied to them. This increases the stability by creating a box-like construction.

Framed structures

Also termed *skeletal* or *skeletion* construction. As its name implies this form consists of an interconnected framework of members, which have a supporting function. The protecting function is carried by either cladding applied to the outside of the framework or infill walls between it. Framed construction is suitable for a wide range of buildings from low to high rise. The actual framework is often pre-made in a factory as separate units, which can be speedily and simply connected on site, as is the case with

Cellular

Cross wall

Figure 6 *Solid structures*

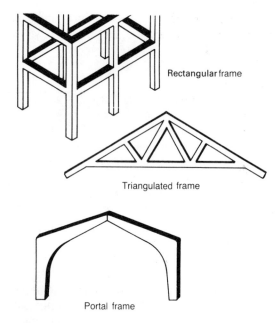

Rectangular frame

Triangulated frame

Portal frame

Figure 7 *Framed structures*

most steel, timber and pre-cast (pre-made) concrete frames. Alternatively, an in situ cast concrete (cast in location) framework may be used, although this method requires the use of formwork (a temporary structure which supports and shapes wet concrete until it becomes self-supporting). The three main types of framed construction are shown in Figure 7, these being *rectangular, triangulated and portal.*

Rectangular framework
This is the most commonly used form of framed construction. It basically consists of a series of vertical supporting members (columns) which are spaced apart and tied together by horizontal spanning members (beams). The resulting framework provides the bearing for floors, walls and roof.

Triangulated framework
This is a framework that has been triangulated or based on the shape of a triangle. This provides a very rigid structure, since the triangle is the most rigid shape possible. The trussed rafter used in pitched roof construction and the

grid structure used for large-span industrial units, are both examples of this form.

Portal framework
A portal consists of a supporting column and roof beam, that are rigidly joined together forming one continuous structural member. These are normally used in pairs bolted together at their apex. Portals are spaced and tied by horizontal members, which also serve as fixing points for the roof sheeting and wall cladding.

Surface structures

These consist of either a thin lightweight material that has been curved or folded to obtain the necessary strength, or a very thin material that is stretched over supporting members or medium. Within these two groups there is a wide variety of forms including, shells, vaults, bent or folded plates, tents and air-supported structures. Surface structures are commonly made from either timber, concrete, steel, plastic, canvas or rubber. A *shell roof* and an *air-supported structure* are shown in Figure 8, and are defined as follows:

Shell roofs
These are normally formed using either in situ cast concrete, or two or three layers of timber boards. The shell illustrated is a combination of

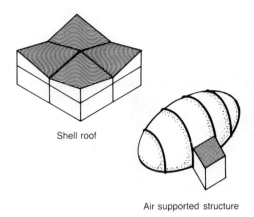

Shell roof

Air supported structure

Figure 8 *Surface structures*

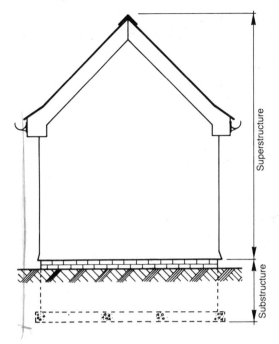

Figure 9   *Substructure and superstructure*

four hyperbolic paraboloids (a shape created by raising the two diagonally opposite corners of a square to a higher level than the other two corners). Because of their lightweight mainly self-supporting nature, shells are suitable for large clear spans-with the minimum of supporting structure.

Air-supported structures

These consist of either a complete skin which is sealed at ground level and supported from the inside by compressed air; or alternatively inflated tubes may be incorporated into the skin to act as supporting ribs. An airlock entry system must be used for the first type of structure. These structures have been used successfully for warehouses, sports complexes and exhibition areas etc.

Structural parts

All structures consist of two main parts: the structure below ground and that above ground.

These are termed the *substructure* and the *superstructure* and are further defined below (see Figure 9):

Substructure

This is all structure below ground, but up to and including the ground-floor slab and damp-proof course. Thus any storeys below ground (basements) are considered part of the substructure. The purpose of the substructure is to receive the loads from the superstructure and transfer them safely down to a suitable load-bearing layer of soil.

Superstructure

This is all structure above the substructure both internally and externally. The purpose of the superstructure is to act as the external envelope and in addition receive the *dead* and *imposed* loads and transfer them safely down onto the substructure.

Dead loads

These can be defined as the self weight of the building materials used in the construction, service installations and any permanent built-in fitments etc.

Imposed loads

These can be defined as the weight of any movable load, such as the occupants of a building, their furniture and other belongings (goods and chattels), and any visitors to the property and their belongings. Also included are any environmental forces exerted on the structure from the external environment (wind, rain and snow).

   Although classified as separate parts, the substructure and the superstructure should be designed to operate as one structural unit.

Structural members

The main parts of a structure which themselves carry a load are said to be in a state of stress (a body subjected to a force). There are three types of stress; see Figure 10.

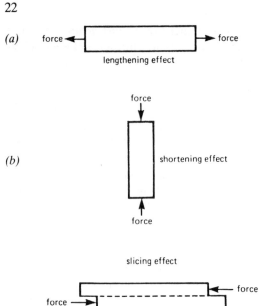

(a) force ← [   ] → force

lengthening effect

(b) force ↓ [ ] shortening effect force ↑

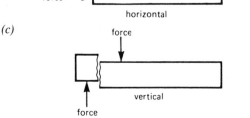

slicing effect

force → [ ] ← force

horizontal

(c) force ↓

vertical

force ↑

Figure 10 *Stress (a) tensile; (b) compressive; (c) shear.*

Compression
This causes squeezing, pushing and crushing; it has a shortening effect.

Tension
This tends to pull or stretch a material; it has a lengthening effect.

Shear
This occurs when one part of a member tends to slip or slide over another part; it has a slicing effect.

The three main types of load-bearing structural members are illustrated in Figure 11, and explained below, these being *horizontal, vertical* and *bracing* members.

Horizontal members
Their purpose is to carry and transfer a load back to its point of support. Horizontal members include beams, joists, lintels and floor or roof slabs etc. When a load is applied to a horizontal member, bending will occur, resulting in a combination of tensile, compressive and shear stresses. This bending causes compression in the top of the member, tension in the bottom

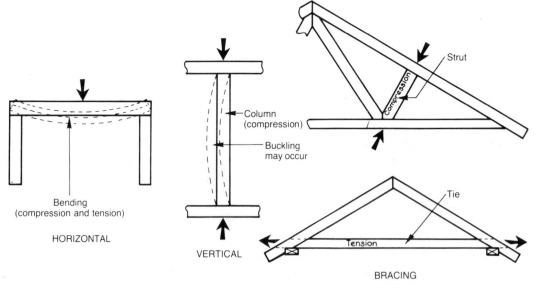

Bending
(compression and tension)

HORIZONTAL

Column
(compression)

Buckling
may occur

VERTICAL

Strut

Compression

Tie

Tension

BRACING

Figure 11 *Structural members*

and shear near its supports and along its centre line. Bending causes the member to sag or deflect. (For safe design purposes deflection is normally limited to a maximum of 3 mm in every 1 m span.) In addition, slender members, which are fairly deep in comparison with their width, are likely to buckle unless restrained (e.g. strutting to floor joists).

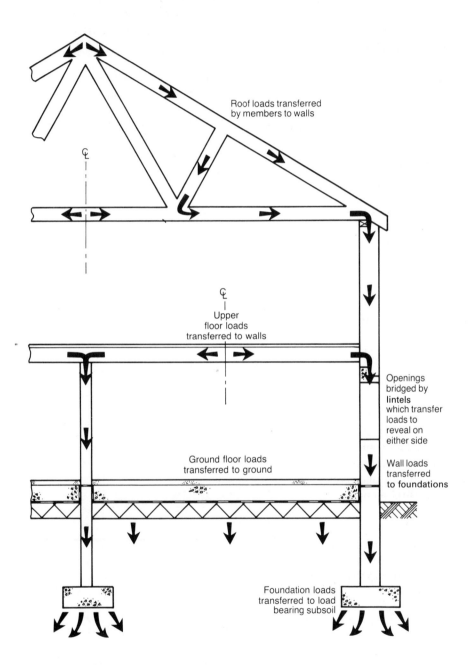

Figure 12   *Transfer of loads*

Vertical members

Their purpose is to transfer the loading of the horizontal members down onto the substructure. Vertical members include walls, columns, stanchions and piers. Vertical members are in compression when loaded. Buckling tends to occur in vertical members if they are excessively loaded or are too slender.

Bracing members

These can be divided into two types: *struts* and *ties*. They are used mainly to triangulate rectangular frameworks in order to stiffen them.

Strut A bracing member that is mainly in compression.

Tie A bracing member that is mainly in tension. At certain times bracing members may, depending on their loading conditions, act as either struts or ties. In these circumstances they may be termed as *braces*.

Examples of loading

An example of dead and imposed loads and how they are transferred down through the structural members to the soil is illustrated in Figure 12.

Self-assessment questions

Question	*Your answer*
1 Name the *three* main structural forms	_____
	_____
	_____
	_____
2 Define crosswall construction	_____
	_____
	_____
	_____
3 Name the term given to a supporting column and roof beam, that are rigidly joined together forming one continuous structural member	_____
	_____
	_____
	_____
4 Sketch the outline of a simple building and indicate on it the substructure and superstructure	

5 Define and state the purpose of the substructure and super-structure

6 Define the terms 'dead' and 'imposed' loads

7 Describe the three types of stress to which structural members may be subjected

8 Describe the difference between a strut and a tie

9 State the term used to describe non-loadbearing external walls

10 With the aid of a sketch, distinguish between cellular and rectangular framework methods of construction

Elements and components

In the previous topic, structures were divided into two main parts, the substructure and superstructure. These may be seen to consist of *elements* which in turn are made up from *components*, e.g. a brick wall is an element, having bricks and mortar as components.

Elements

An *element* can be defined as a constructional part of either the substructure or superstructure havings its own functional requirements. These include the foundations, walls, floors, roof, stairs and the structural framework or skin. Elements may be further classified into three main groups: *primary elements, secondary elements* and *finishing elements*.

Primary elements

These are named because of the importance of their supporting, enclosing and protection functions. In addition, are their mainly internal functions of dividing space and providing floor-to-floor access. Typical examples of primary elements are shown in Figure 13, and described as follows:

Foundations

The part of the structure (normally in situ concrete) that transfers the dead and imposed loads of the structure safely onto the ground. The width of a foundation will be determined by the total load of the structure exerted per square metre on the foundation and the safe load-bearing capacity of the ground, e.g. wide foundations for either heavy loads or weak ground and narrow foundations for light loading or high-bearing capacity ground. The load exerted on foundations is spread to the ground at an angle of 45 degrees. Shear failure leading to building subsidence (sinking) will occur if the thickness of the concrete is less than the projection from the wall/column face to the edge of the foundation. Alternatively, steel reinforcement may be included to enable the load to be spread across the full width of the foundation (see Figure 14). Foundations are taken below ground level to protect the structure from damage resulting from ground movement. The actual depth below ground level is dependent on a number of factors: load-bearing capacity of the ground, need to protect against ground movement and tree roots etc. In most circumstances, a depth of one metre to the bottom of the foundation is considered to be the minimum.

Ground movement is caused mainly by the shrinkage and expansion of the ground near the surface owing to the wet and dry conditions. Compact granular ground suffers little movement whereas a clay (cohesive) ground is at high risk. Frost also causes ground movement when the water in the ground expands on freezing. This is known as frost heave and is limited to about 600 mm in depth. The main problem with tree roots is shrinkage of the ground owing to the considerable amounts of water they extract from it. Tree roots can extend out in all

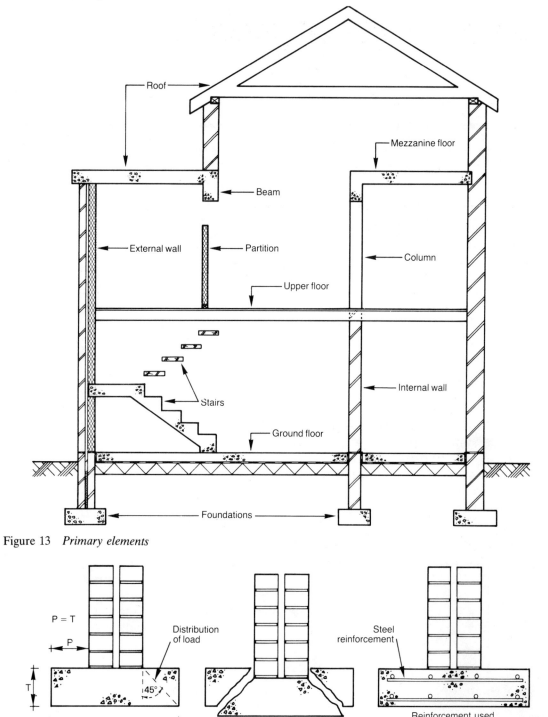

Figure 13   *Primary elements*

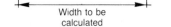

Figure 14   *Foundation size*

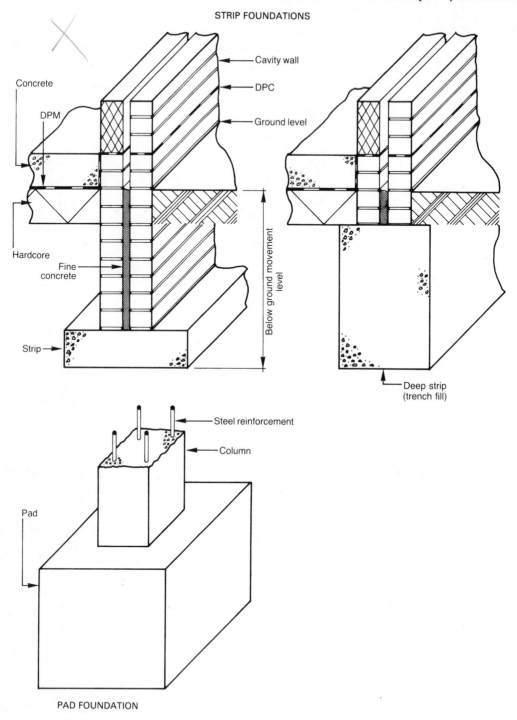

Figure 15   *Types of foundations*

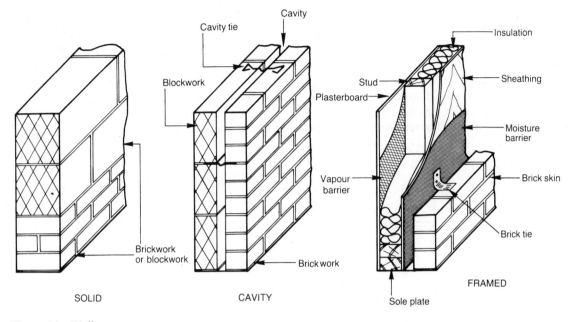

Figure 16 *Walls*

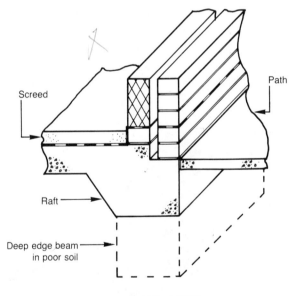

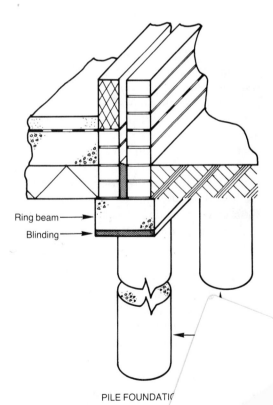

Figure 15 *continued*

directions from the base of a tree greater than its height.

The four most common types of foundations are strip, pad, raft and pile (see Figure 15). For most small-scale building works strips are commonly used for solid structures and pads for frame structures, except where the subsoil is of a poor unstable quality. In these circumstances, a raft or piles would be more suitable.

Walls

The walls of a building may be classed as either load bearing or non-load bearing. In addition, external walls have an enclosing role and internal walls a dividing one. Thus load-bearing walls carry out a dual role of supporting and enclosing or dividing. Internal walls, both load and non-load bearing are normally termed *partitions*. Openings in load-bearing walls (windows and doors) are bridged by lintels which support the weight of the wall above.

Walls may be divided into three main groups according to their method of construction (see Figure 16). These are *solid, cavity* and *framed*.

Solid walls These are made from bricks, blocks or concrete. When used externally, very thick walls are required (450 mm or over) in order to provide sufficient thermal insulation and prevent rain being absorbed through the wall to the inside (causing internal dampness etc.) before heat and air circulation can evaporate it from the outside. Because of the costs involved the method is now rarely used. An alternative method is to use thinner external solid walls (normally insulating blocks) and apply an impervious (waterproof) surface finish to the outside, e.g. cement rendering.

Cavity walls These consist of two fairly thin walls or leaves (about 100 mm each) separated by a 50 mm to 75 mm cavity. The cavity prevents the transfer of moisture from the outside to the inside and also improves the walls' thermal-insulation properties. Therefore they are in common use for the low to medium-rise enclosing walls of dwellings. The standard form

of the wall is a brick outer leaf and an insulating block inner leaf, or as an alternative, a timber-framed inner leaf. To reduce heat transfer through the wall, it is fairly common practice to fill the cavity with a thermal-insulating material (mineral wool, Fibreglass, foam or polystyrene etc.).

Framed walls These are normally of timber construction and are made up in units called *panels*. They may be either load- or non-load-bearing and also for use externally or internally. They consist of vertical members which are called *studs* and *horizontal members*, the top and bottom of which are called the head and sole plates whilst any intermediates are noggins.

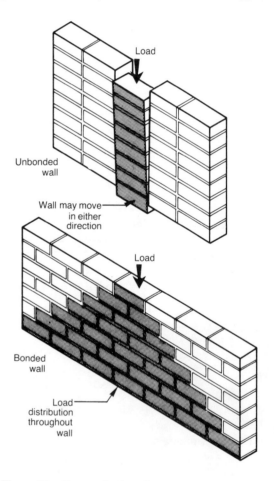

Figure 17   *Reason for bonding*

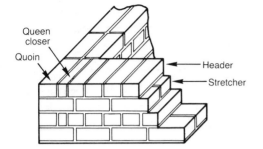

ENGLISH BOND

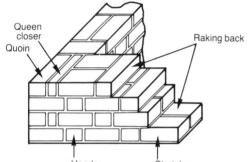

FLEMISH BOND

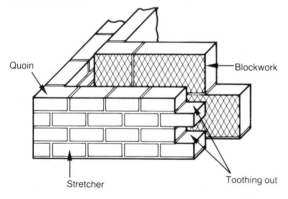

STRETCHER BOND

Figure 18 *Bonding*

Bonding The strength of brickwork is dependent on its bonding (overlapping of vertical joints). This is necessary to spread any loading evenly throughout the wall (see Figure 17).

Solid walls are normally built in either *English or Flemish bond*. English bond consists of alternate rows (courses) of bricks laid lengthways along the wall (stretchers) and bricks laid widthways across the wall (headers). Flemish bond consists of alternate stretchers and headers in the same course. In both, the quarter lap is formed by placing a queen closer (brick reduced in width) next to the quoin (corner brick). See Figure 18.

Cavity walls are built in stretcher bond where all bricks show their stretcher faces, although adjacent courses overlap by half a brick. To ensure sufficient strength, the inner and outer leaves are tied together across the cavity at intervals with cavity ties. See Figure 18.

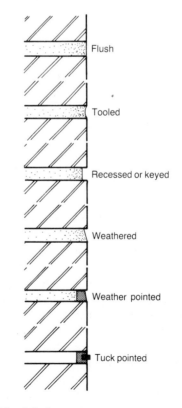

Figure 19 *Jointing*

Their thermal- and sound-insulating properties are greatly improved by filling the spaces between the members with mineral wool or fibreglass etc. Sheathing may be fixed to one or both sides of the panel to improve strength. This type of wall panel is used in the majority of present-day timber-frame house construction as the internal leaf of the cavity wall.

Jointing Brickwork and blockwork walls are jointed by means of mortar (mixture of sand and cement and/or lime forming an adhesive). Horizontal joints are known as bed joints and vertical ones as perpends or perps. The face of these joints may be finished in a variety of profiles, which are intended to improve the weathering resistance and appearance of the work. See Figure 19.

Cladding External walls are sometimes co-vered over with boarding, tiles, or other material; this is known as *cladding*. It is used for either decorative purposes, weatherproofing purposes or both. Cement rendering is often used as an alternative to cladding also providing a decorative weatherproofed finish.

Floors

These may be divided into two groups: *ground floor* and *upper floors*. The main functions of a floor is to provide an acceptable surface, insulation and carry and transfer any loads imposed upon it. In addition, ground floors are also required to prevent moisture penetration and weed growth.

Ground floors There are two types of ground-floor construction: *solid* and *suspended* or *hollow*. A solid ground floor is in direct contact with the ground and a suspended one spans from wall to wall as illustrated in Figure 20.

SOLID GROUND FLOORS These are built up from a number of layers. Hardcore provides a suitable base for the construction. A thin blinding layer of sand or weak concrete is often used to fill voids or level out the rough edges of the hardcore in order to reduce grout loss or the risk of puncturing the damp-proof membrane (DPM). The DPM is placed between the hardcore and concrete slab to prevent dampness rising through the floor. It is essential that that DPM is lapped into the walls' damp-proof course (DPC) in order to prevent any possibility of ground moisture bypassing the DPM. The concrete floor slab (also known as the oversite concrete

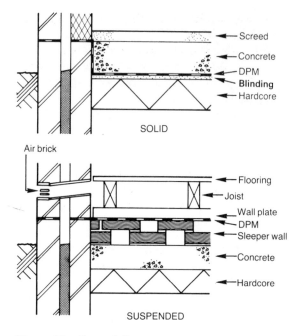

Figure 20   *Ground floors*

since it covers the whole site of the building) is not built into the walls but acts as an independent raft transferring its imposed loading direct-ly to the ground and not the foundations. For industrial use, warehouses and garages etc., the concrete may form the actual floor finish. In other buildings, it is normal to lay a cement and sand screed. This screed levels the slab, takes out any irregularities and provides a smooth surface to receive the final floor finish, e.g. carpet, lino, tiles, woodblocks or strips etc.

SUSPENDED GROUND FLOORS In common with solid ground floors, these still require the hardcore and oversite concrete layers. The dwarf or sleeper walls which support the timber floor construction are built on top of the oversite at about 1.8 m centres using honeycomb bond (a bond that leaves half-brick voids in the wall to allow air circulation). Air bricks must also be included in the outside walls at ground level to enable through ventilation in the under-floor space. This prevents the moisture content of the timber rising too high. (Timber in poorly ventilated areas with a moisture content above

20% will almost inevitably be attacked by dry-rot fungi.)

The timber-floor construction consists of floor boards or sheets, supported by joists that bear on wall plates which in turn spread the load evenly along the sleeper walls. A DPC is placed between the wallplate and sleeper walls to prevent the rise of ground moistures into the timber work.

Upper floors These are also known as suspended floors (see Figure 21). Timber construction is mainly used for house construction and concrete for other works.

TIMBER-SUSPENDED FLOORS These consist of a number of bridging joists supported at either end by load-bearing walls. The joists are covered on their top by floor boarding or sheeting to provide the floor surface and on their bottom with plasterboard to form the ceiling. The end of the joists may be supported by building them into the internal leaf of the cavity wall.

Alternatively, they may be supported on metal joist hangers, which have a flange that locates in the joint of the wall. Where openings in the floor are required for stairs etc., the joists must be framed or trimmed around the opening. This entails cutting short a number of bridging joists so that they do not protrude into the opening. These are called trimmed joists. Trimmer and trimming joists, which are thicker than the bridging, are framed around the opening to provide support for the ends of the trimmed joists. In order to prevent joists longer than 2 m buckling when under load, they must be strutted at their centre. This strutting has the effect of stiffening the whole floor.

CONCRETE-SUSPENDED FLOORS These are supported on the walls or structural framework. They may be formed using either reinforced in situ cast concrete or some form of precast units. In both cases, the top surface will require screeding to receive the floor finish and the bottom surface will need plastering or another form of finishing to provide the ceiling surface.

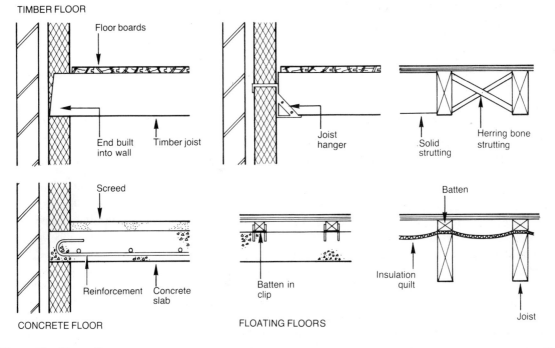

Figure 21 *Upper floors*

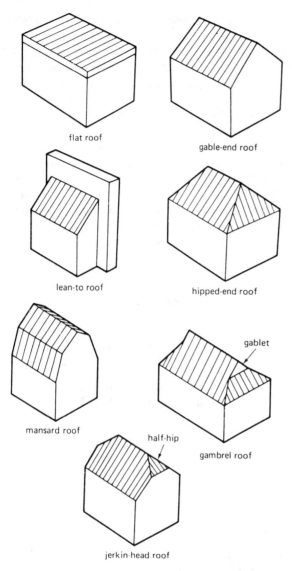

Figure 22   *Roof types*

top of it. Their main purpose is to form a discontinuous structure and thus improve a floor's sound insulation.

Roofs

Roofs are part of the external envelope that spans the building at high level and has weathering and insulation functions. They are classified according to their pitch (slope of the roof surface) and also their shape, the most common of which are illustrated in Figure 22. A glossary is given below:

Flat roof   This is one where the slope or pitch of the roof surface does not exceed 10 degrees.

Pitched roof   This is where the slope or pitch of the roof surface exceeds 10 degrees. These may be further divided into a number of types:

    Lean-to   This is a single or monopitched roof (only one sloping surface)

    Gable-end roof   This is a double-pitched roof (having two sloping surfaces) terminating at one or both ends with a triangular section of brickwork.

    Hipped-end roof   A double-pitched roof where the roof slope is returned around the shorter sides of the building to form a sloping triangular end.

    Mansard roof   A double-pitched roof where each slope of the roof has two pitches. The lower part has a steep pitch, while the upper part rarely exceeds 30 degrees. May be finished with either gable or hipped ends.

    Gambrel roof   A double-pitched roof having a small gable or gablet at the ridge and the lower part a half-hip.

    Jerkin-head roof   A double-pitched roof which is hipped from the ridge part way to the eaves, and the remainder gabled.

Flat roofs   The basic construction of flat roofs (Figure 23) is very much like that of either timber or concrete upper floors, but with the addition of firring pieces (long wedge-shaped pieces fixed on top of the joists) or a sand and

The in situ concrete floor will require the erection of formwork to cast and support the wet concrete. In general, concrete floors are more airborne, sound-resistant and have better fire-resistant properties than do timber floors.

Floating floors   These consist of battens and floor boarding that are independent of the structural floor, simply resting or 'floating' on

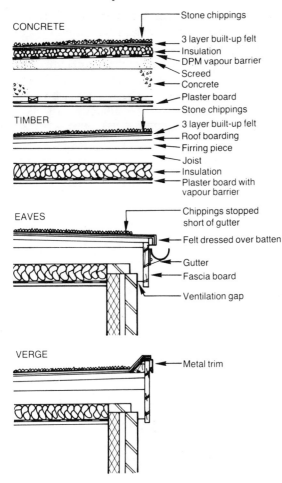

CONCRETE
— Stone chippings
— 3 layer built-up felt
— Insulation
— DPM vapour barrier
— Screed
— Concrete
— Plaster board

TIMBER
— Stone chippings
— 3 layer built-up felt
— Roof boarding
— Firring piece
— Joist
— Insulation
— Plaster board with vapour barrier

EAVES
— Chippings stopped short of gutter
— Felt dressed over batten
— Gutter
— Fascia board
— Ventilation gap

VERGE
— Metal trim

Figure 23 *Flat roof details*

rafters are supported in mid-span by a beam called a *purlin*. The overhanging edges of a roof are called *eaves* where they are level and *verge* when sloping. The piece of timber that finishes these edges is called a *fascia board* at the eaves and a *barge board* at the verge; both may be closed on the underside with a soffit board.

The type of roof covering is governed by the pitch of the roof. In general, as the pitch lowers, the unit size of the covering material must increase. If the pitch is too slack for the covering, water can make its way through the joints between the covering by capillarity and find its way into the building. Table 2 gives minimum pitches for some roof coverings.

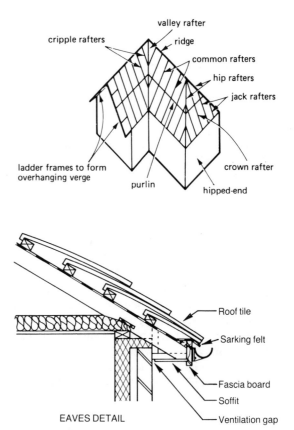

cripple rafters
valley rafter
ridge
common rafters
hip rafters
jack rafters
ladder frames to form overhanging verge
purlin
crown rafter
hipped-end

cement screed. These provide the slight fall towards the guttering to dispose of the rainwater. The most common covering materials are built-up felt and bitumin adhesive or sheet metal for timber flat roofs and asphalt for concrete ones.

Pitched roofs   Pitched roofs (Figure 24) consist of rafters variously named according to their position, most of which span from a wall plate at the lower end to a ridge board at their apex. Rafters support the tile battens which in turn provide a fixing for the tiles or slates. Sometimes

— Roof tile
— Sarking felt
— Fascia board
— Soffit
EAVES DETAIL
— Ventilation gap

Figure 24 *Pitched roof: terminology and eaves detail.*

Table 2 **Minimum roof pitches**

Material	Minimum pitch (degrees)
Corrugated sheets	12
Interlocking tiles	22.5
Large slates	25
Plain tiles	35
Pan tiles	35
Thatch	45
Small slates	45

A variety of roof tiles and a slate are illustrated in Figure 25. Every slate must be secured with two aluminium, copper or zinc nails. Tiles only require nailing about every fourth course, as they have nibs which hang over the battens and hold them in place. Also shown in Figure 25 is a half-round tile that is bedded in cement mortar and used to cover the open ridge and hip joints.

An untearable sarking felt is fixed on top of the rafters below the covering material. This is to prevent the penetration of wind-assisted rain and snow into the building. Water may find its way through the joints of the tiles or slates otherwise. This felt should extend down over the fascia into the eaves gutter to drain any water collected.

Where roofs abut walls or chimney stacks etc., the joint must be weatherproofed to prevent moisture penetration. Metal flashings are used for this purpose.

Stairs

The function of stairs is to provide floor-to-floor access. They can be defined as a series of steps (combination of tread and riser), each continuous set of steps being called a *flight*. Landings may be introduced between floor levels, to break up a long flight giving rest points, or to change the direction of the stair. Stairs can be classified according to their plan shape as shown in Figure 26 or by the material from which they are made. Timber stairs are common in dwelling houses, whilst concrete is most common for other purpose groups.

A typical timber flight consists of treads and risers, housed into strings, the outer one of which is joined to newel posts. These support the hand rails and balusters that protect the side of a flight and are collectively called the *balustrade*. The triangular space under a flight, called the *spandrel*, is often filled in to form a cupboard (see Figure 27).

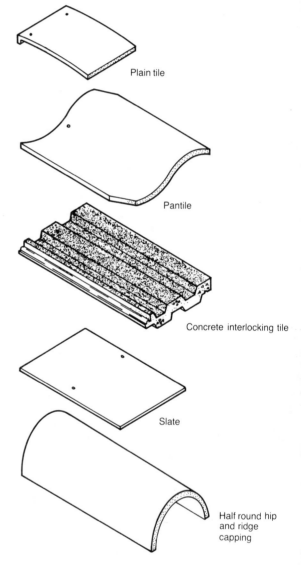

Plain tile

Pantile

Concrete interlocking tile

Slate

Half round hip and ridge capping

Figure 25   *Pitched roof coverings*

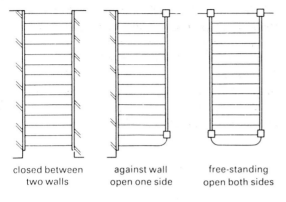

closed between   against wall   free-standing
two walls   open one side   open both sides

(a)

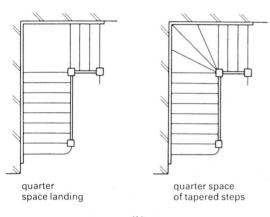

quarter   quarter space
space landing   of tapered steps

(b)

Secondary elements

These are the non-essential parts of a structure which have a mainly completion role around openings in primary elements and within the building in general. Typical secondary elements are shown in Figure 28 and described as follows.

Doors, frames and linings

The function of a door opening is to permit access into, and between, the various areas of a building. A door is a movable barrier intended to seal the opening and provide privacy, security and insulation. The main types of door are *flush, panelled, glazed* and *matchboarded*, as illustrated in Figure 29.

Doors can be hung on either frames or linings. In general, frames (which are fairly large rectangular sections) are used for external and other heavy doors, whilst linings (which are much thinner) cover the full width of the wall and are used for internal doors (see Figure 30).

Windows

The main function of windows is to admit air and daylight into the building and give its occupants a view outside. Windows are normally classified by their method of opening as illustrated in Figure 31. These are: *casements* which are top or

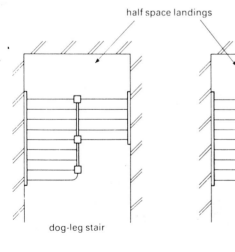

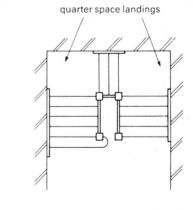

half space landings   quarter space landings

dog-leg stair   open newel stairs

(c)

Figure 26   *Stairs. (a) Straight-flight; (b) quarter-turn; (c) half-turn.*

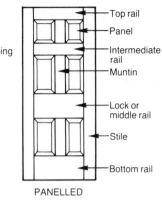

FLUSH   PANELLED

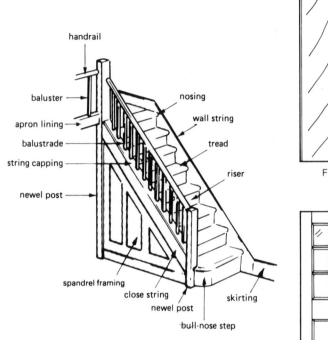

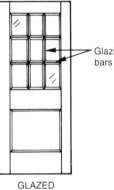

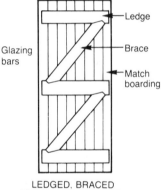

GLAZED   LEDGED, BRACED
AND MATCH BOARDED

Figure 27   *Stairway terminology*

Figure 29   *Doors*

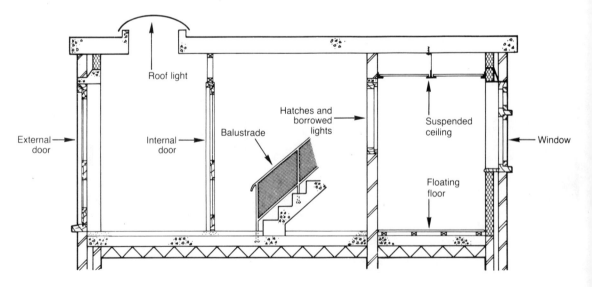

Figure 28   *Secondary elements*

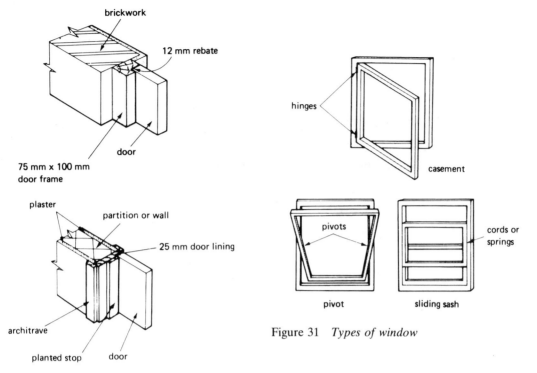

Figure 30   *Door frame and lining*

Figure 31   *Types of window*

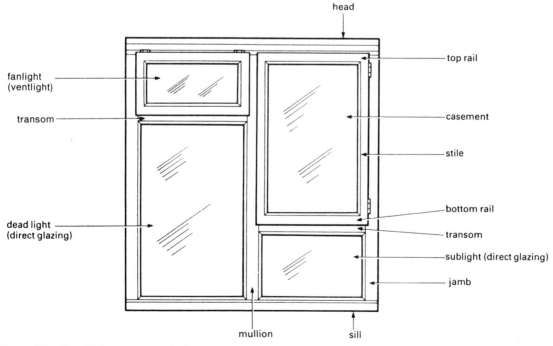

Figure 32   *Four light casement window*

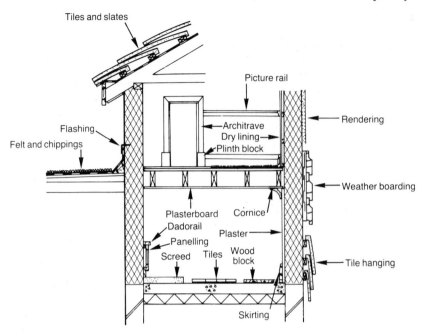

Figure 33   *Finishing elements*

side hung on hinges; *pivot* hung either horizontally or vertically and sliding sashes either horizontally or vertically.

Casement windows   These are the most common type in use, and consist of two main parts (Figure 32).

The frame   This consists of head, sill and two jambs. Where the frame is subdivided, the intermediate vertical members are called *mullions* and the intermediate horizontal member is called a *transom*.

The opening casements   These consist of top rail, bottom rail and two stiles. Where the casement is subdivided, both the intermediate vertical and horizontal members are called *glazing bars*. Opening casements which are above the transom are known as *fanlights*. Fixed glazing is called a dead light and glazing at the bottom of the window, normally below a casement is a sublight. Where glass is bedded in the main frame itself, it is called direct glazing.

Windows which project beyond the face of a building are known as a *bay*; those which project from an upper storey only are an *oriel*; those with a continuous curve are a *bow*. Windows that contain a pair of casements for giving access to a garden or balcony are called *French*.

Finishing elements

A finish is the final surface of an element which can be a self finish as with face brickwork or an applied finish such as wallpaper and paint. Typical examples of finishing elements are shown in Figure 33. Included in this category are internal trims (skirting, architraves and coving or cornices) which mask the joint between adjacent elements and external flashings which weatherproof the joint.

Components

The primary elements, secondary elements and services of a building are made up invariably from a number of different parts or materials; these are known as *components*. Examples of three main types of components are shown in Table 3 and are defined as follows:

Section components A section is a material that has been processed to a definite cross-sectional size but of an unspecified or varying length, e.g. a length of timber.

Unit components A unit is a material that has been processed to a definite cross-sectional size and length, e.g. a brick.

Compound components These are combinations of sections or units put together to form a complex article, e.g. a window frame.

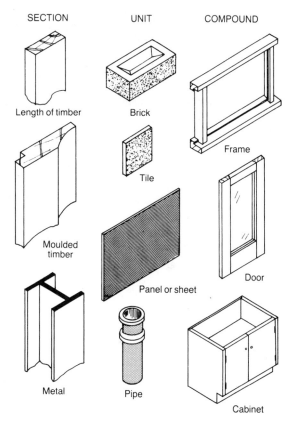

Table 3

Self-assessment questions

Note: Your response to all multiple-choice items should be recorded by filling in the line under the appropriate letter with an HB Pencil thus:

a   b   c   d

Question	Your answer
1 Define the terms primary, secondary and finishing elements	

2 State to which of the above
elements the following be-
long: (i) paint; (ii) external
wall; (iii) plaster; (iv) door;
(v) roof

_____

_____

_____

_____

3 State *two* functions of a
ground floor

_____

_____

_____

_____

4 Use labelled sketches to show
the difference between
(i) solid ground floor and
(ii) suspended ground floor

5 State the difference between
section, unit and compound
components

_____

_____

_____

_____

6 State *one* example for each of
those in question 5.

_____

_____

_____

_____

7 Name the timber component
that closes the eaves of a roof

_____

_____

_____

_____

8 State *two* advantages cavity
walls have over solid walls

_____

_____

_____

9 The finishing element that weatherproofs the joint between adjacent elements is called:
   (a) weathering
   (b) cladding
   (c) rendering
   (d) flashing?

   ⊏ a ⊐   ⊏ b ⊐   ⊏ c ⊐   ⊏ d ⊐

10 The intermediate vertical component part of a door is a:
   (a) muntin
   (b) stile
   (c) rail
   (d) mullion?

   ⊏ a ⊐   ⊏ b ⊐   ⊏ c ⊐   ⊏ d ⊐

Services

In order to produce the required conditions (clean, hygienic and comfortable etc.), services are added to the structure. Services can be grouped under two main headings: *basic* and *specialist*.

Basic service installations

Certain basic services are considered as essential requirements for all buildings. They are normally provided by statutory undertakings which operate on either local, regional or on a national basis, these being:

Water This is for drinking, washing, heating, cooking, waste/soil disposal and industrial processes.

Electric This is for lighting, heating, cooking, cleaning, air-conditioning, entertainment, telecommunications and industrial processes.

Gas This is for heating, cooking and industrial processes.

Drainage This is for the disposal of waste water and sewage.

These basic services consist of systems of pipes and wires which are either fixed within, or on, the surface of the elements. They are connected to the public supply usually via a meter which records the amount used. Each undertaking has its own set of regulations concerning the supply, use of, and any alterations to, its service. These regulations must be complied with when provision is made within a building for connection to the particular service.

Water supply

Water undertakings have to provide a sufficient supply of wholesome drinking water to all buildings. In order to do this, they must collect and reclaim water for treatment (filtration, sterilization and sometimes softening). It is then stored until required by consumers, where distribution is through a mains water pipe. This service is paid for by means of a water rate levied on all properties. Industrial and other bulk users of water may have a water meter installed.

Water mains are situated at least 900 mm below ground and usually follow the line of the roads. They are made of either asbestos cement, cast iron, steel or PVC. Connection to the property is via a communication/service pipe (copper, PVC or polyethylene). The communication pipe runs from the mains up to a stop valve in a protection chamber adjacent to the boundary. A goose neck or expansion bend is incorporated in the communication pipe to relieve any stress likely on the connection owing to settlement. From the stop valve the service pipe continues into the building and terminates just above ground-floor level with a stop valve and drain-down valve. A minimum cover of 750 mm is recomended for the service pipes; where the pipe passes through the substructure it should be housed in a protective pipe duct. This arrangement is shown in Figure 34.

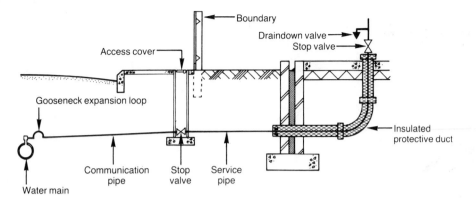

Figure 34   *Water supply*

Cold-water systems
From the stop valve within the building, the supply of *cold water* may be via either a direct or indirect system.

Direct cold-water system   In areas where there is a good supply and pressure of water, a direct system (Figure 35) may be permitted. In this, all pipes to the cold draw-off points are taken direct from the service pipe. The only stored water required is a small storage cistern to feed the hot-water system.

Indirect cold-water system   In the indirect system (Figure 36) the service pipe (rising main) has only one draw-off point to supply drinking water at the sink; otherwise it goes directly to the cold-water storage cistern. This is positioned

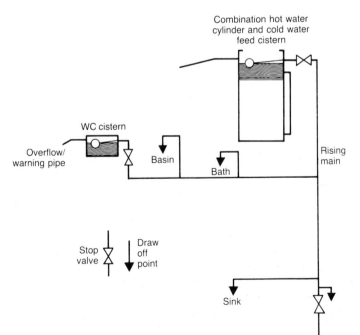

Figure 35   *Direct cold water system*

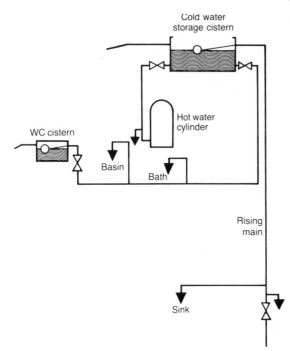

Figure 36   *Indirect cold water system*

cylinder; a gas circulator connected to the cylinder; a gas or solid-fuel back boiler; or by means of an independent boiler fired by gas, solid fuel or oil. Like cold water, both direct and indirect systems are used.

Direct hot-water system   In this system (Figure 37) the cold water flows through the boiler or circulator where it is heated. As a result of heating, convection currents are set up, causing the hot water to rise to the cylinder and be replaced by colder water by gravity. Alternatively, it may be heated directly in the cylinder by an immersion heater. Hot water is drawn off the top of the cylinder, and is distributed to the draw-off points by a supply pipe, which also continues vertically to discharge over the cold-water storage cistern (which acts as a vent or expansion pipe). As hot water is drawn off, the cylinder is topped up directly from the cold-water cistern. This type of system is not suitable for use in hard-water areas or where radiators for heating are required, as this will cause lime

at high level (normally in the roof space) to ensure sufficient 'head' or pressure of water. All of the remaining cold water draw-off points are supplied from the cistern as is the feed to the hot-water system.

In both systems, the supply of water is controlled by stop valves at various points; these allow the water to be shut off from different parts of the system. The level of water in the cisterns is controlled by a ball valve which shuts off when it floats to the required level. Overflow pipes are also provided to cisterns to safely discharge water should the ball valve fail to shut off.

Hot-water systems

The supply of *hot water* to domestic fittings is normally taken from the top of the hot-water cylinder which is supplied from the cold-water storage cistern. The source of heat may be one, or a combination of, the following alternatives: an electric immersion heater fitted into the

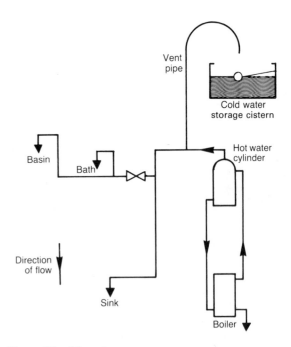

Figure 37   *Direct hot water system*

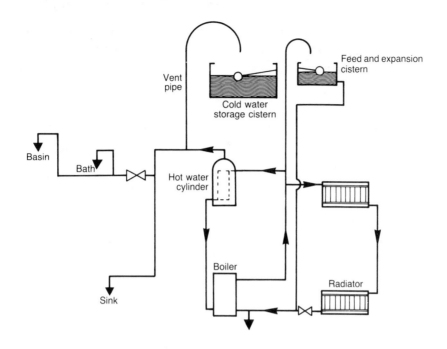

Figure 38 *Indirect hot water system with radiators*

furring in the pipework and cylinder and corrosion in the radiators.

Indirect hot-water system This system (Figure 38) is intended to overcome the problems of furring and corrosion by not constantly introducing fresh cold water into the boiler circuit. The water still circulates between the boiler and cylinder but as it passes through a coil within the cylinder, it does not mix with the water that may be drawn off. The hot water passing through the coil heats the cold water in the cylinder, from where it is distributed in the same manner as the direct hot-water system. A small additional cold-water cistern is required for the initial supply of the boiler and to top up any losses owing to evaporation. In addition, an expansion pipe from the boiler is also set over this cistern.

Copper is generally used for the pipework of both cold- and hot-water systems, capillary joints and hot-water cylinders. Storage cisterns are usually either galvanized mild steel or plastic. Control valves etc. are mainly brass.

Thermal insulation
Although not a service, thermal insulation is essential if heating costs are not to be wasted. Figure 39 illustrates the percentage heat losses through the various building elements of a typical house. Considerable savings in heat loss can be achieved by thermally insulating the building elements and the hot-water fittings (see Figure 40.). As heat rises, the roof space is normally the first to be insulated. This is also the most cost-effective area (quickly repaying the cost of insulation by savings in heating bills).

The roof space can be insulated by laying either Fibreglass, mineral wool, expanded polystyrene or vermiculite between the ceiling joists. The cold-water storage tanks should be lagged to prevent them freezing in the winter, although as an extra precaution the tank will be kept warmer if the ceiling insulation is not continued under them.

Cavity walls where not already filled with insulation during the building process can have insulating material injected into them. This may

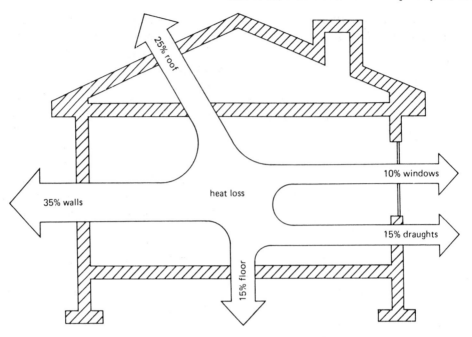

Figure 39   *Heat loss*

be either a plastic foam, polystyrene granules or mineral wool fibre. Solid walls can be improved by adding an internal insulating layer. This may take the form of a cavity by lining the walls with foil-backed plasterboard on battens. Extra benefit is achieved by filling the space between battens with fibreglass or mineral wool.

Sealed-unit double glazing is most effective against heat loss through windows and glazed doors. Secondary double glazing, although normally not so good, will stop draughts but both are expensive. A simple and fairly cheap method of cutting down on heat loss through draughts around windows and doors is to fix sealing strips around their joints and over postal flaps.

Ground floors are rarely additionally thermally insulated because they lose the least heat of any element, coupled to the fact that heat rises. If required however the insulation of hollow ground floors may be improved by laying fibreglass or mineral wool between the joists and suspended on wire mesh. A floating floor finish

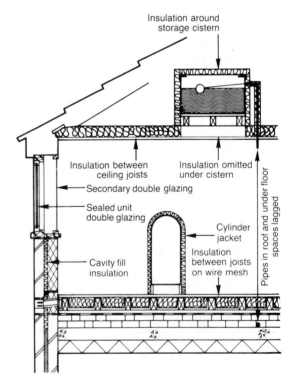

Figure 40   *Thermal insulation*

with insulation between the battens may be used to improve solid ground floors.

Electric supply

Electricity is a form of energy which is produced by generating equipment at power stations. These generators may be powered by coal, oil, or gas turbines or a nuclear reactor. The power of flowing water may also be used to drive these generators (hydro electricity). The Central Electricity Generating Board is responsible for the generation and primary distribution of electricity, while area boards handle the regional and local distribution and supply of electricity to individual properties.

Electricity from the generators is supplied into the national grid (network of overhead cables on pylons) at very high voltages (electric pressure). This is transformed down in voltage and fed into the regional grids, which consist of both overhead and underground cables. Substations in the regional grid again reduce the voltage to suit the power requirements of the user.

Electricity from the grid is brought into a building to the meter position either by an overhead service cable from the Board's supply pole (common in rural areas) or an underground service cable connected to the Board's main, which is situated under the road. The service cable terminates at a sealed fuse unit which is connected via two short lengths of cable (live and neutral) to the meter fixed alongside. Electricity flows through the live wire and in order to complete the circuit returns along the neutral. In addition, an earthing connection is provided to an earth clamp, earth rod or an earth leakage circuit breaker. Some properties have a second meter which operates through a sealed time switch, to record the utilization of offpeak (cheaper) electricity.

Connection is made from the meter to the consumer unit (often called fuse box) which

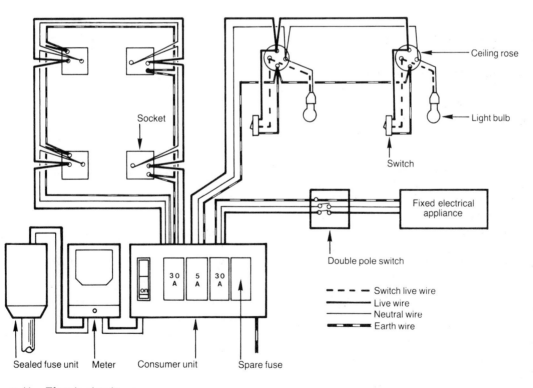

Figure 41 *Electric circuits*

incorporates a mains switch that can cut off the electricity to all the circuits and a number of fuses or miniature circuit breakers (MCBs) to protect the individual circuits. The fuse or MCB is the weakest link in the circuit; its purpose is to cut off the supply should an overload or fault occur (fuses contain a wire that melts and MCBs have an automatic trip-switch). The consumer unit is also connected to the earthing terminal. Domestic properties normally use three types of circuit (Figure 41).

Lighting circuit
There is usually one circuit for each floor level.

Ring main power circuit
Socket outlets are provided for portable electrical appliances, again usually one circuit for each floor level.

Radial power circuit
These are individual circuits for fixed electrical appliances.

Each circuit consists of a cable with two conductor wires (live and neutral) and an earth wire (all normally copper or aluminium), surrounded by an insulator (often plastic). This cable may link together a number of lights or socket outlets or run direct to the control box of the fixed appliance. Where the circuit is continuous, (the cable at both ends connects to the consumer unit), it is known as a *ring main system*. Others which connect at one end only are called *radial circuits*. Ring main systems evenly distribute the load on the electrical circuit at any one time. Radial circuits are used to supply power to a limited area, say a garage, or for fixed appliances. Sometimes a radial circuit may be 'spured' off a ring main to supply a single socket outlet.

Modern three flat-pin plugs used to connect portable appliances contain a cartridge fuse. The rating of the fuse is related to the rating of the appliance (look on the rating plate, usually on the back or base). Appliances rated up to 700 watts require a 3 amp fuse, those rated over this (and up to 3 kilowatts) require a 13 amp fuse.

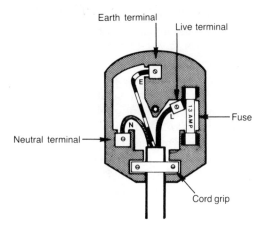

Figure 42   *Wiring a plug*

Remember that voltage is electrical pressure, amps (or amperes) measure the rate of current flow and a watt is the unit of power, which is equal to volts multiplied by amps (1 kilowatt = 1000 watts).

The cable on a portable appliance is normally of a three-core type, which must be correctly wired up in accordance with the colour code. The cable on older appliances may contain:

A green earth flex
A red live flex
A black neutral flex

Modern appliances will have the new international colour-coded cable which consists of:

A green and yellow striped earth flex
A brown live flex
A blue neutral flex

These flexes *must* be connected to the correct terminals of the plug (see Figure 42):

Green or green and yellow flex to the terminal marked earth, E or ⏚

Red or brown flex to the terminal marked live or L

Black or blue flex to the terminal marked neutral or N

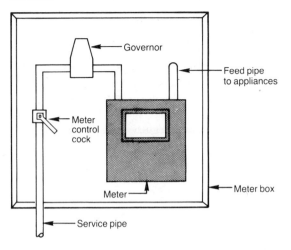

Figure 43   *Gas meter*

Gas supply

Gas is a combustible fuel which is supplied via a network of trunk and distribution mains, normally situated under the roadway or footpath. Most of the gas now used is natural gas (North Sea gas). This supply is provided by the area gas boards under the guidance of the Gas Council. In locations where piped gas is not available, bottled propane or butane gas can be used.

The gas supply from the mains to individual properties is via an underground service pipe (normally bright yellow plastic) to the point of entry where it runs either through the substructures and terminates just above floor level in the meter position with a control cock, or to an external meter box again terminating with a control cock. Adjacent to the control cock is a governor to stabilize the gas pressure and the meter which measures the volume of gas used (see Figure 43).

Gas is distributed to the various appliances by mild steel or copper pipes. Most appliances have an individual control cock, enabling them to be disconnected from the supply for servicing. Gas cookers are often connected using a flexible hose which is simply plugged into a bayonet-type fitting. This arrangement allows the easy removal of the cooker for cleaning.

Drainage systems

The purpose of drainage systems is to collect soil, waste and surface water and discharge it efficiently (normally by gravitational forces) into a public sewer. These public sewers are normally sited under roads and are maintained by the Water Board/local authority, for which service, including the later treatment of the water, a rate is levied. In areas where public sewers are not available, other means of disposal can be used, e.g. cesspools and septic tanks.

Soil water   This is the term used to describe human excrement, urine and the water used to flush the system, e.g. water discharged from water closets (WCs) and urinals.

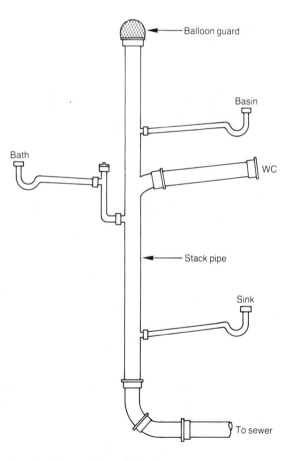

Figure 44   *Single-stack drainage system*

Waste water   This is the flow of water from baths, sinks, wash basins and showers.

Surface water   This is rainwater collected from roofs and other hard areas (paths, drives etc.).

Above-ground drainage

In modern construction, both soil and waste water (known as foul water) are normally collected into a single vertical stack pipe (termed single-stack system). This stack is located within the building for protection. It will connect to the underground drain at its lower end and continues up above the roof with an open end providing ventilation to the whole system (see Figure 44). Discharges from the ground floor are normally connected independently to the drains. The pipes that connect baths, sinks, wash basins and showers to the stack are known as waste pipes. Older properties may have a two pipe

system both external, one stack for the soil and another for the waste.

Surface water from the roof is normally collected in a gutter fixed to the eaves; vertical down-pipes known as rainwater pipes (RWPs) take the water to the drain, where connection is made via a back-inlet gully; older properties may have a grated gully and rainwater shoe (Figure 45). Water from hard areas may be allowed to 'run off' and soak into the ground or be collected in grated gullies, which are connected to the drainage system.

Below-ground drainage

The actual layout of the underground drainage system depends on the type of sewerage system in use; in some areas the foul and the surface water discharge into separate sewers, these being the foul-water sewer (FWS) and the surface-water sewer (SWS). This is known as a separate system. Foul water must be treated at a sewerage purification works whereas surface water is allowed to discharge into rivers and the sea. In other areas, a combined system may be used, where both the foul and surface water are discharged into a single sewer. Although only one sewer is required, costs are increased as all of the water must be treated.

Sometimes soakaways are used to collect the surface water. These are pits dug in the ground, filled almost to the top with coarse hardcore and topped up to ground level with soil. The surface-water drain discharges into this pit which allows the water to percolate into the surrounding soil.

Inspection chambers (ICs) (often called manholes) are provided where drains meet and at sharp bends. These permit access for both inspection and the clearing of blockages. The actual connection to the sewer may be made by a Y-shaped junction, a saddle which is a curved back fitting that sits over a hole in the top of the sewer, or an inspection chamber.

The plan and typical elevation of a drainage system for a detached house is shown in Figure 46. In this system, foul water is taken to the FWS, surface water from the house roof is

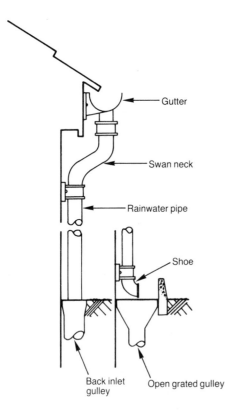

Figure 45   *Roof drainage*

Table 4 Drainage and sanitary materials†

Material	Application												
	Basins	Baths	Drain pipes	Gutters	Inspection chamber	RWPs	Showers	Sinks	Stack pipes	Urinals	Waste pipes	WCs	WWPs
Aluminium				*		*							
Brickwork					*								
Cast iron		*	*	*		*	*		*				*
Concrete			*		*								
Copper											*		
Earthenware			*	*		*			*				
Lead			*	*		*			*		*		
Plastic	*	*	*	*	*	*	*	*	*		*		*
Pressed steel (coated in vitreous china)	*	*					*	*					
Stainless steel	*						*	*		*			
Vitreous china	*						*	*		*		*	*

†RWPs = rainwater pipes; WCs = water closets; WWPs = waste-water preventer.

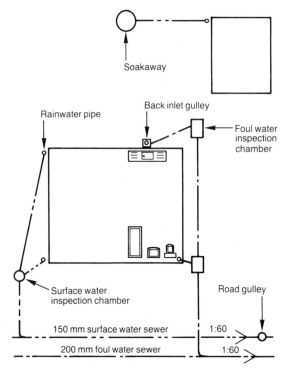

Figure 46   *Below-ground drainage system*

An overflow pipe from the WWP is taken through an outside wall where it will be noticed if the ball float valve sticks and the overflow drips. The remaining sanitary appliances are normally provided with water by means of taps connected to the hot and cold supplies. An overflow is provided near the top of waste appliances; this discharges water directly into the waste pipe or trap, thus preventing overfilling of the appliance.

Materials used for drainage and sanitary appliances are listed in Table 4.

Specialist service installations

In addition to the basic services which have been covered in this topic other specialist service installations are associated with specific building usage or types of structure. These include: lift installations, escalators, sprinkler systems, security systems, refuse-disposal systems, cable television systems, clocks, telephones, computer facilities and other communication systems etc.

discharged into the SWS, while that from the garage is drained into a soakaway. The road drainage gullies also discharge into the SWS. In addition, the direction of sewage flow and the gradient of the sewers is indicated.

Sanitary appliances

Two types of sanitary appliances are used: those which receive soil (WCs and urinals); and those which receive waste (baths sinks, wash basins and showers). All sanitary appliances either incorporate a water trap within themselves or have one incorporated in the waste or soil pipe that connects them to the drain (see Figure 47). This trap is designed to prevent any foul drain smells entering back into the building through an appliance.

After use, WCs are flushed with cold water to carry away the soil. The water is provided by a, hand-operated cistern (sometimes called a WWP or waste-water preventor) which is immediately refilled through a ball float valve.

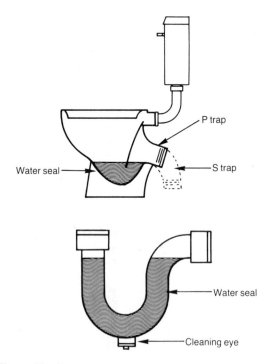

Figure 47   *Water traps*

Self-assessment questions

Question   *Your answer*

1 Name the *four* basic services
  which are considered essential for all buildings
  _____

  _____

  _____

  _____

2 Distinguish between direct
  and indirect systems of cold-
  water supply
  _____

  _____

  _____

  _____

3 State where in a domestic
  house drinking water can be
  obtained
  _____

  _____

  _____

  _____

4 Produce a single-line sketch
  to show an indirect hot-water
  system

5 (i) State the purpose of thermal insulation and (ii) name
  the most cost-effective area in
  a house to insulate; suggest a
  method
  _____

  _____

  _____

  _____

6 Describe and state the purpose of a ring main power
  circuit
  _____

  _____

  _____

  _____

7 Define the following:
  (i) National grid; (ii) volts;
  (iii) MCB; (iv) spur

8 Sketch a three flat-pin plug,
  with its top removed, clearly
  indicating the fuse, terminals
  and the colour of the flexes
  connected to them

9 Describe how drain smells
  are prevented from entering
  back into a building through
  sanitary appliances

10 Distinguish between soil,
   waste and surface water

Topic 5

Materials

There is a wide range of materials both natural (timber and stone) and manufactured (bricks, metal and plastics) which are available to the building designer. The actual selection of a particular material for a specific purpose will depend on the following points of consideration. Materials must

1 satisfy the client's requirements both functionally and aesthetically
2 satisfy these requirements over the expected life of the building, with the minimum of maintenance
3 be readily available at a cost that comes within the client's budget
4 comply with relevant British Standard specifications and codes of practice, and other statutory building controls, e.g. Town and Country Planning, Building Regulations and service undertakings (electric, water, gas, etc.)
5 blend in with the local environment in such a way that, as far as possible, they are aesthetically acceptable to all concerned

The main groups of building materials along with their constituents, uses and appearance are described and/or illustrated in the following section. Where appropriate, the excepted drawing symbol for materials is given in Figure 48.

Adhesives

These are substances that are used to bond other materials together. Bonding is obtained by mechanical adhesion, specific adhesion or both.

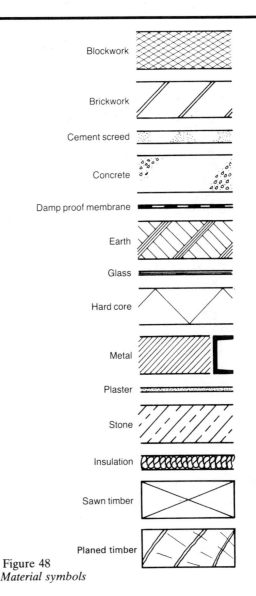

Blockwork

Brickwork

Cement screed

Concrete

Damp proof membrane

Earth

Glass

Hard core

Metal

Plaster

Stone

Insulation

Sawn timber

Planed timber

Figure 48
Material symbols

Mechanical adhesion is where the adhesive penetrates the materials surface and keys into the porous or roughened layers.

Specific adhesion occurs where smooth materials are in very close contact.

Most adhesives are applied as a liquid. In order to develop cohesive strength (strength within themselves) they must change from their liquid state to a solid state. This takes place during the setting and curing either by loss of solvent, cooling, chemical reaction or a combination of these processes. Adhesives are classified as either *natural* or *synthetic* (typical uses are shown in brackets).

Natural

These include animal glue made from bones and hide (timber); casein which is derived from soured, skimmed milkcurds (timber); bituminous which is based on bitumen or coal tar (roofing felt); rubber contact adhesive (plastic laminates).

Synthetics

These are of two types. Thermoplastics set by loss of solvent or cooling but can be softened again if the solvent or heat is reintroduced. An example is PVA (polyvinyl acetate) (timber, leather, cloth, paper; also as a bonding agent for plaster, mortar and floor screeds). Thermosetting synthetics undergo a chemical reaction on setting and cannot be dissolved or melted. Examples are phenol or resorcinol formaldehyde (laminated structural timber (Glulam), external plywood) and epoxy resins (almost all materials). (See also p. 64.)

Aggregates

Aggregates are granular materials which are bonded together into a single mass. By using different types of aggregate and bonding agents, materials with differing properties, colours and surface textures can be formed.

Aggregates may be termed as:

Fine aggregate (sand) All of its grains will pass through a 5 mm sieve. Those with angular grains are called sharp sands while those with rounded or smooth grains are called soft sand.

Coarse aggregate (gravel and crushed rock) None of its grains will pass through a 5 mm sieve.

All-in aggregate A well-graded mixture of fine and coarse aggregates.

Lightweight aggregate Having a density of not more than $1200 \, kg/m^3$ for fine aggregates and not more than $1000 \, kg/m^3$ for coarse.

Natural aggregates Naturally occurring materials, e.g. gravel, sand and crushed rock.

Manufactured aggregate Mostly created as a by-product of some industrial processes often involving heat, e.g. blast furnace slag, pulverized fuel ash, exfoliated vermiculite and expanded perlite.

The uses of aggregates are in mortars, concrete, hardcore, insulation, plaster and tar macadam.

Bituminous products

These comprise bitumen, coal tar and pitch. They are extremely resistant to the passage of water and are normally black, dark brown or red in colour.

Bitumen can either be natural or distilled from petroleum and is used for mastic asphalt, paints, adhesives, roofing felt and damp-proof courses.

Coal tar is used with aggregate for tar macadam and is also suitable for many bitumen applications.

Pitch, which is derived from coal tar, is used mainly for pitch mastic flooring and pitch fibre drain pipes.

Blocks

A building block (Figure 49) is a walling unit

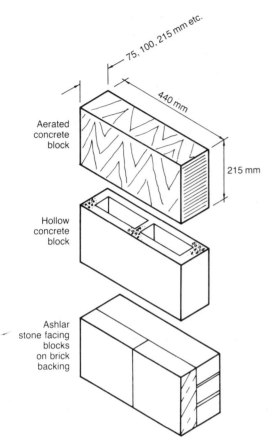

Figure 49   *Blocks*

mortar) or covered in cladding (tiles, slates or timber etc.). Concrete blocks are termed dense or lightweight. Lightweight blocks use either a lightweight aggregate or a fine aggregate mix that is aerated to form air bubbles.

Bricks

Bricks (Figure 50) are a walling unit component. Their standard format size including an allowance for the mortar jointing is 225 mm × 112.5 mm × 75 mm high. After deducting the mortar allowance, this makes the actual size of the brick 215 mm × 102.5 mm × 65 mm. The two main categories of bricks are *clay* and *calcium silicate*, according to the material used in their formation. Clay bricks are pressed, cut or moulded and then fired in a kiln at very high temperatures. Their density, strength, colour and surface texture etc. will depend on the variety of clay used and the kiln temperature. Some bricks have their surface dressed with sand to improve their appearance, although this is easily chipped off during the building process.

Calcium silicate bricks are either sandlime or flintlime, lime being the bonding agent and sand or flint being the aggregate. They are pressed and steamed at a very high temperature,

component which is larger than a brick but still small enough to be handled and layed in much the same way as bricks. The most common material for blocks is concrete. Stone blocks are also available although they are expensive and thus rarely used for new work, except as a dressed stone facing known as ashlar fixed to a brickwork or concrete backing. Blocks are most often used for internal walls or the inner leaf of cavity walls.

The main advantage of blocks over bricks is good thermal-insulation qualities and their increased speed of laying (because of their greater size and fewer joints). When used externally, because of their appearance and protecting properties, they are normally rendered (covered with a thin layer of cement

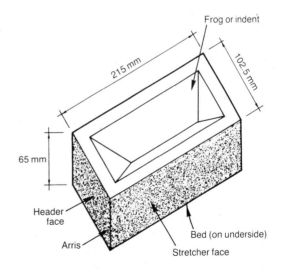

Figure 50   *Brick*

producing a brick that is more regular than clay ones, although in general they are not as strong or durable. Pigments may be added during the manufacturing process to achieve a range of colours.

Bricks are also further classified according to their variety, durability and type. They are of three varieties:

Common or Fletton bricks

These are not chosen for their appearance or strength. They are a basic brick used in the main, for internal or covered (rendered or cladding) external work, although sand-faced flettons are often used as a cheap facing brick.

Facing bricks

These are made from selected clays and chosen for their attractive appearance rather than any other characteristic.

Engineering bricks

These have a very high density and strength and do not absorb moisture. They are thus ideal for use in both damp conditions (inspection chambers, basements and other work below ground) and highly loaded conditions (substructure of tall buildings or column supporting a beam).

Clay bricks are classified for their durability (frost resistance and soluble salt content).

Frost resistant (F) are durable in all situations.

Moderately frost resistant (M) are durable except when saturated and subjected to repeated freezing and thawing.

Not frost resistant (O) are recommended for internal use only.

Low soluble salts (L) are for use in exposed conditions.

Normal soluble salts (N) are liable to cause efflorescence (white powdery stain on the face of brickwork caused by the surfacing of soluble mineral salts).

Based on the previous classifications, bricks may be obtained with the following durability designations: FL, FN, ML, MN, OL and ON.

There are *four* types of brick:

Solid A brick having no holes, cavities or depression.

Perforated A brick having holes passing through it, up to 25% of its gross volume.

Frogged A brick with a depression in one or both of its bed faces, which in total are up to 20% of its gross volume.

Cellular A brick where depressions or cavities exceed 20% of its gross volume.

The purpose of both frogs and perforations is to increase the strength of the bond between the brick and mortar joint.

Boards, slabs and sheets

These are used extensively in construction (Figure 51). Many are timber based; they range from low-strength fibreboard wall linings and insulation, to very strong plywood used for structural purposes. In the following examples, main uses are included in brackets.

Plywoods Usually consist of an odd number of thin timber layers glued together with their grains alternating (flooring, formwork, panelling, sheathing, cabinet construction).

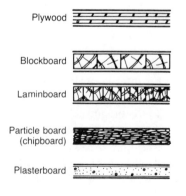

Figure 51   *Sheet material*

Laminated boards Consist of strips of timber which are glued together, sandwiched between two veneers (panelling, doors, cabinet construction).

Particle boards Mainly known as chipboard, is manufactured from wood chips and flakes impregnated with an adhesive (flooring, furniture, cabinet construction).

Fibre boards Made from pulped wood, mixed with an adhesive and pressed forming hardboard, medium board, and insulation board (floor, wall, ceiling and formwork linings, insulation, display boards).

Woodwool slabs Made from wood shavings coated with a cement slurry (roof decks, permanent formwork).

Plastic laminate Made from layers of paper impregnated with an adhesive (work tops and other horizontal and vertical surfaces requiring decorative, hygienic and hard-wearing properties).

Plasterboard Comprises a gypsum plaster core sandwiched between sheets of heavy paper (wall and ceiling linings).

Cement

Cement is one of the most widely used materials. It is manufactured from chalk or limestone and clay which are ground into a powder, mixed together and fired in a kiln causing a chemical reaction. On leaving the kiln, the resultant material is ground to a fine powder. Hence a popular site term for cement is 'dust'.

When water is added to the cement, another reaction takes place causing it to gradually stiffen, harden and develop strength. The commonest type of cement is called *Ordinary Portland Cement (OPC)* not because it comes from that area, but when hardened its appearance resembles Portland stone. Other types of cement are used in specific circumstances:
Rapid Hardening Portland Cement (RHPC) for cold weather use.

Sulphate Resisting Portland Cement (SRPC) for use underground in high sulphate conditions.
White or Coloured Portland Cement, made using white china clay; pigments are added for coloured cements.
High Alumina Cement (HAC). This uses bauxite (aluminium oxide) instead of clay. It develops very early strength which is much higher than OPC, although in the long term it has been found unstable and thus now rarely favoured for structural work.

Cement is used in all forms of in situ and pre-cast concrete products, cement mortar, cement screeds, rendering.

Ceramics

Ceramics consist of a mixture of sand and clay which has been shaped, dried and finally fired in a kiln. This results in the formation of a hard, smooth surface, glassy material. Ceramics are available in any colour. This is achieved by coating them with a prepared solution before firing.

The main types of ceramic are:

Terracotta is used mainly for unglazed air bricks, chimney pots and floor tiles.

Faience is a glazed form of terracotta and stoneware.

Fireclay, having a high fire resistance, is used for firebacks and flue linings.

Stoneware is more glassy than fireclay and is used for underground drainage goods.

Earthenware is normally white, has fine texture and a highly glazed surface. Used for wall tiles.

Vitreous china is more glassy than earthenware and is used for sanitary appliances.

Concrete

Concrete (Figure 52) is comprised of cement, fine and course aggregates and water. When these materials are mixed together, the fine aggregate fills the voids in between the coarse aggregate. The cement mixes with the water and

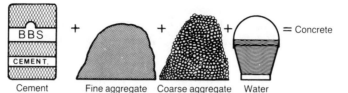

Figure 52   *Concrete*

coats the surfaces of the aggregate, bonding them together. The concrete then sets by a chemical reaction between the cement and the water.

Concrete mixes are normally specified by volume. A typical specified mix might be 1:3:6. This means:

1 part Portland cement
3 parts fine aggregate
6 parts coarse aggregate

The amount of water used in the mix should be kept to the minimum required to provide a workable mix. This is because, as the amount of water increases above the minimum, the strength of the concrete decreases.

Concrete rapidly increases in strength during this initial curing process (setting). It will have obtained 85% of its strength after 28 days, and will continue to gain the remaining 15% of its strength during the rest of its life. Concrete is inherently very strong when used in compression, although where tensile forces are present it should be reinforced with steel to prevent cracking and ultimate failure.

Glass

The basic constituents of glass are sand, soda ash, limestone and dolomite. These are heated in a furnace to produce molten glass. Additional ingredients can be added to produce a glass with special properties. On cooling the molten mixture becomes hard and clear. Flat glass can be produced by a number of different processes:

Spunglass
This method was used right up to the 19th Century. Molten glass was blown into a balloon shape, and spun round, forming a disc of glass called a *crown*. This was cut up into pieces and set into lead strips. The centre piece of the crown was thick and had a circular mark in it from the spinning process. This was called *bullion glass* and sold off cheaply.

Drawn glass
In use from the mid-19th Century onwards. Molten glass is drawn up between rollers in a continuous flow, cooled in water towers and cut into sheets. Patterned rollers may be introduced to create rough cast and patterned glass. Wire can be incorporated in the glass during the drawing to form wired glass. The surfaces of drawn glass are not perfectly flat; this causes distorted vision. Thus large sheets of glass for shop fronts etc. had to be ground and polished perfectly flat to give undistorted vision. This type of glass is known as *polished plate*.

Float glass
This gives an undistorted vision without the need for polishing. It is made by floating the molten glass onto the surface of liquid tin, and subsequently allowing to cool.

Mastics

These are rubber, bitumen or plastic-based sealing compounds, which are used in modern buildings to seal joints around the outside of windows and door frames, against rain, air and sound, while still allowing differential movement between the two materials. These mastics are normally sold in tubes for use in guns which have a nozzle at one end through which the mastic is extruded.

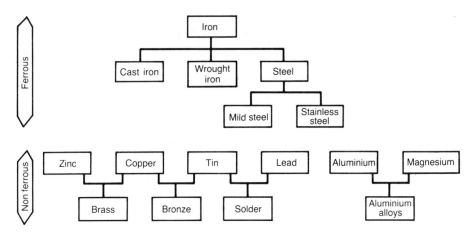

Figure 53   *Metals*

Metals

Metals (Figure 53) are minerals; very few are found as such in nature. Most have to be extracted from metallic ores by either smelting in a furnace and/or electrolytic methods. All metals are classified as being either ferrous or non-ferrous.

Ferrous metals

These are all extracted from iron ore with varying amounts of carbon added to them, e.g. wrought iron, cast iron, mild steel, high-tensile steel. They will corrode rapidly when exposed to air and water, until they are completely rusted. Chromium and nickel may be added to form a stainless-steel alloy that is resistant to rusting.

Non-ferrous metals

These do not contain iron. They consist of other principal metals, e.g. zinc, copper, tin, lead, aluminium and magnesium, that corrodes very slowly when exposed to sulphur-containing gases or solutions and carbon dioxide which are present in the air. This corrosion forms a film on the surface which can protect the metal against further corrosion. In general, the principal non-ferrous metals are rather soft and are often mixed in their molten form to produce harder alloys; e.g. zinc and copper are mixed to form brass; copper and tin form bronze; tin and lead form solder; aluminium and magnesium for aluminium alloys.

Mortar

Mortar is the gap-filling adhesive that holds bricks, blocks or stonework together to form a wall. It takes up the slight difference in shape and provides a uniform bed to transfer the loads from one component to the next. The four main types of mortar are mixtures of the following with water; typical mix proportions are shown in brackets.

Cement – sand mortar	(1:3)
Lime – sand mortar	(1:3)
Cement – lime – sand mortar (known as compo mortar)	(1:1:6)
Cement – sand plus plasticizer mortar	(1:6)

Cement mortars are stronger and more resistant to moisture than lime mortars. Lime is added to cement mortar to reduce its tendency to crack whilst improving workability and bonding properties. Plasticizers are used as an alternative to lime for improving the workability of mortars.

Paint

Paint is a thin decorative and/or protective coating which is applied in a liquid or plastic form and later dries out or hardens to a solid film covering a surface.

Paints consist of a film former, known as the vehicle; a thinner or solvent (water, white spirit or methylated spirit, etc.) to make the coating liquid enough; and a pigment suspended in the vehicle to provide covering power and colour.

Paint schemes require either the application by brush, spray or roller, of one or more coats of the same material (varnish, emulsion and solvent paints) or a build up of different successive coats, each having their own functions (primer, undercoat and finishing coat).

Varnish A paint without a pigment, used for clear finishing.

Emulsion A water-thinned paint for use on walls and ceilings.

Solvent paint Based on rubber, bitumen or coal tar and used for protecting metals and water-proofing concrete etc.

Primer May form a protective coat against moisture and corrosion, or act as a barrier between dissimilar materials. Also provides a good surface for subsequent coats.

Undercoat A paint used on primed surfaces to give it a uniform body and colour on which a finishing coat can be successfully applied.

Finishing coat This seals the surface, gives the final colour and provides the desired surface finish (flat, egg-shell, gloss).

Plaster

This is the material applied on internal walls and ceilings to provide a jointless, smooth, easily decorated surface. External plastering is normally called *rendering*. Plaster is a mixture that hardens after application; it is based on a binder (gypsum, cement or lime) and water with or without the addition of aggregates. Depending on the background (surface being plastered) plastering schemes may require the application of either one coat, or undercoats to build up a level surface followed by a finishing coat. The main plasters in use are:

Gypsum plaster

For internal use different grades of gypsum plaster are used according to the surface and coat. Undercoats, use browning for general use and bonding for concrete; finishing coats, use finish on an undercoat or board finish for plasterboard.

Cement–sand plaster

This is used for external rendering, internal undercoats and water-resisting finishing coats.

Lime–sand plaster

This is used for both under and finishing coats (rarely), although lime can be added to other plasters to improve their workability.

Lightweight aggregates such as expanded perlite and exfoliated vermiculite can be added to plasters giving them good thermal and *fire-resisting* properties.

Plastics

Plastics are synthetic (man-made) materials which are derived mainly from petroleum and also coals. Plastic products are formed into their required shape while the solution is still in its soft state, by a variety of processes including extrusion through a shaped die, film blowing into a tube, sheet casting onto a cooled surface, and injection or vaccum forming into a mould. Two distinct groups of plastics can be identified: *thermoplastics* and *thermosetts*.

Thermoplastics

These can be softened by heat and will re-harden on cooling. In general, they tend to be soft, easily scratched and have little resistance to loading, although they have good moisture-resistance properties. Typical examples in building are:

Acrylic for baths and basins, showers and sheets.

Nylon used for door and window fittings.

Polythene for damp-proof courses and membranes, waste pipes, water pipes and tanks.

Polyvinyl chloride (PVC) used for electrical insulation, sheets and floor tiles. Unplasticized or rigid PVC known as UPVC is used for soil pipes, waste pipes and gutters.

Polystyrene used for tiles and insulation.

Thermosetts

These undergo a chemical change when setting and cannot be resoftened appreciably by heat. In general, they are harder and stronger than thermoplastics. In addition, they have good electrical insulation properties. Typical examples used in building are:

Phenol, resorcinol, urea and melamine formaldehyde resins which are used for adhesives and electrical fittings.

Polyester reinforced with a glass fibre to form glassfibre reinforced plastic (GRP).

Polyurethane for foam products and mastic sealants.

Stone

Natural stones or rocks are used extensively in building, for walling, roofing, paving and tiling. They may be classified into *three* groups; *igneous*; *sedimentary*; and *metamorphic*.

Igneous stones

These were formed by the original solidification of the earth's molten material (magma). They are extremely hard wearing and strong in compression. Granite is the main building example.

Sedimentary stones

These were formed by a sedimentary or settling process, whereby rock and organic particles were deposited, often on the seabed, in successive layers which subsequently compacted to form a solid. Sandstone and limestone are the main examples. Being sedimentary, they can contain hard and soft layers which weather at different rates.

Metamorphic stones

These were formed from older stones that had been subjected to very high temperatures and pressures, which caused a structural change to take place. The two main examples are *marble* which was formed from limestone, and *slate* formed from clay.

Thermal insulators

A wide range of materials are added to a building with the purpose of restricting the transfer of heat through the element by conduction. Materials that are poor conductors are good insulators. Still air is a very good insulator; in fact most thermal insulators are basically air traps. Typical thermal insulators used in construction are:

Fibreglass

This is glass strands woven in sheets or rolls used for wall and roof insulation.

Polystyrene

Polystyrene is an air expanded plastic resin made in sheets or loose fill for walls and roofs.

Rock fibre

A woven rock fibre is also called *mineral wool*, for wall, roof and fire insulation.

Vermiculite

This is a flaky mineral which is expanded or exfoliated at a high temperature, used as a loose fill for roofs. Also added as a lightweight aggregate to concrete and plaster, improving their thermal insulation and fire-resisting properties.

Timber

Owing to its strength, low weight, durability, ease of working and wide availability, timber is one of the most versatile and important building materials. *Timber* is an organic material that is produced during the growth process of a living tree. Trees are divided into two groups: *softwoods* (coniferous) and *hardwoods* (broadleaf). This grouping has nothing to do with the hardness of the timber concerned, but is based solely on its structure. Biologically, softwoods have a simple two-type cell structure (tracheids and parenchyma) whereas hardwoods are more complex, consisting of three types of cells (fibres, parenchyma and pores). Examples of timber are:

Hardwoods: beech, oak, mahogany and teak.

Softwoods: pine, spruce, and fir.

In general, softwoods are less decorative than hardwoods and tend to be used for structural work and painted joinery and trim. Hardwoods are more often used for decorative work, polished joinery and trim.

Material information sources

There is a wide range of information available on materials, components and methods of incorporating them into a building. The following is a selection of these sources.

1 Building Regulations.
2 British Standards Institution
   British Standard Specifications and Codes of Practice
3 Building Research Establishment
   BRE Digests, information papers and current papers

4 Research, manufacturers and trade development associations:

   Agrément Board
   American Plywood Association
   Brick Development Association
   British Woodworking Federation
   Building Centre
   Cement and Concrete Association
   Chipboard Promotion Association
   Copper Development Association
   Council of the Forest Industries of British Columbia
   Fibre Building Board Development Organization
   Finnish Plywood International
   Forestry Commission
   Lead Development Association
   Swedish and Finnish Timber Council
   Timber Research and Development Association
   etc.

Copies of their publications are normally available for student reference in most college libraries. Many libraries also take trade periodicals, which operate a readers' enquiry service whereby technical brochures and information can be obtained from various manufacturers and suppliers. In addition, they may even have one of the many product-information systems, e.g. Barbour Index, RIBA Product Data, Building Products Index or Specification etc.

Self-assessment questions

Question   *Your answer*

1 List *four* points of consideration when selecting materials
   for a specific purpose

2 Name and distinguish between the *two* distinct groups
of plastics

_____

_____

_____

_____

3 With the aid of a sketch
describe laminboard

4 State *two* circumstances
where the use of engineering
bricks would be considered

_____

_____

_____

_____

5 Identify the materials from
the following abbreviations:
(i) OPC; (ii) PVA (iii) GRP;
(iv) UPVC; (v) HAC

_____

_____

_____

_____

6 A typical concrete mix is
specified as 1:3:6. Describe
what this means

_____

_____

_____

_____

7 State the reasons for adding
lime to cement mortars and
plasters

_____

_____

_____

_____

8 State the main property that
  most thermal insulators have
  in common

  _____

  _____

  _____

  _____

9 Describe the difference between a varnish and a gloss
  finishing paint

  _____

  _____

  _____

  _____

10 The graphical drawing symbol shown in Figure 54 repre-
   sents:
   (a) brickwork
   (b) blockwork
   (c) stonework
   (d) sawn timber

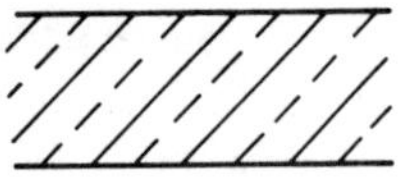

Figure 54 *Self-assessment question*

Faults, defects and failures

It is an accepted fact that all buildings will deteriorate (develop faults and defects which if not rectified may lead onto failures) to some extent as they age. This deterioration may even start as the individual components are incorporated into the building elements during the construction process. In certain circumstances the deterioration of the components may have started either prior to their delivery to the building site or during their storage, before the commencement of construction operations.

The rate and extent to which a building deteriorates is dependent on one or more of the following main factors: *maintenance*; the *environment*; *design and construction*.

Maintenance

This is taken to mean the keeping, holding, sustaining, or preserving of a building and its services to an acceptable standard. This may take one of two forms, *planned maintenance* or *unplanned maintenance*.

Planned or routine maintenance

This is a definite programme of work aimed at reducing to a minimum the need for often costly unplanned work. It includes the annual inspection and servicing of general plumbing, heating equipment, electrical and other services etc.; the periodic inspection and cleaning out of gutters, gullies, rainwater pipes and airbricks etc; the periodic redecoration, both internally and exter-

nally; the routine general inspection/observation of the building fabric and moving parts; finally, also included under this heading, is what is known as preventive maintenance. Basically this is any work carried out as a result of any of the previous inspections in anticipation of a failure, e.g. the early repair or replacement of an item, on the assumption that minor faults almost certainly lead onto bigger and more costly faults unless preventive work is carried out.

Unplanned emergency or corrective maintenance

This is work that is left until the efficiency of the element or service falls well below the acceptable level or even fails altogether. This is the most expensive form of maintenance, making inefficient use of both labour and materials and often also creating serious health/safety risks, and is the type most often carried out. This is because the allocation of money to enable maintenance work to be planned is given low priority.

Environmental factors

These include the deterioration of components and finishes owing to chemical pollution in the atmosphere; the effect of the elements (weather) on the structure, e.g. frost, rain, snow, sun and the wind; the effect of these elements when allowed to penetrate into the building; the deterioration of components owing to biological attack (fungal decay and insect attack).

Design and construction factors

Faulty design and construction methods can lead to rapid deterioration of a building. In fact over 30% of all maintenance/repair could be avoided if sufficient care is taken at the design and construction stages.

Faulty design

This results from inadequate knowledge or attention to detail on the part of the architect or designer, leading to, for example, poor specification of materials/components, structural movement, moisture penetration, biological attack and the inefficient operation of the buildings services.

Faulty construction

Inadequate supervision during the construction process can result in poor workmanship, the use of inferior materials and the lack of attention to details/specifications. These can all lead to the same problems as those stated for faulty design,

resulting in subsequent problems and expense for the building owner.

Agents of deterioration

Apart from the natural ageing process of all buildings during their anticipated life (however well maintained), deterioration of buildings can be attributed directly to one or often a combination of the following agents: *dampness, movement, chemical attack* and *biological attack*.

Dampness

Dampness in buildings is the biggest single source of trouble. It causes the rapid deterioration of most building materials, can assist chemical attack and creates conditions which are favourable for biological attack. Dampness can arise form three main external sources: *rain penetration, rising damp* and *condensation*. In addition, leaking plumbing and heating systems and spillage of water in use are also significant causes of dampness.

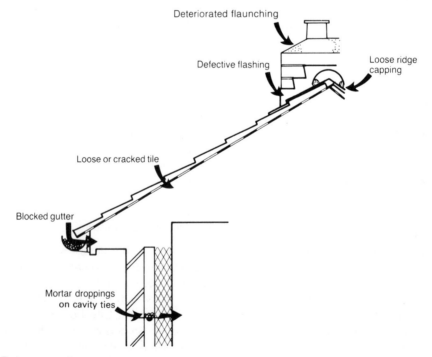

Figure 55   *Rain penetration*

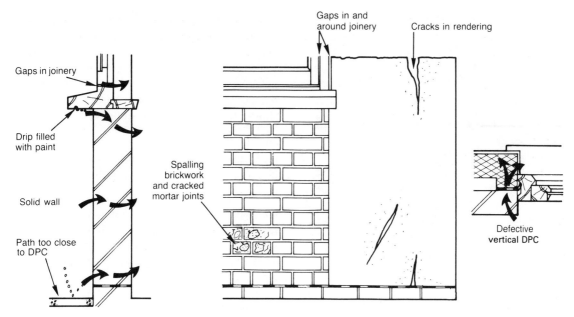

Gaps in joinery

Drip filled
with paint

Solid wall

Path too close
to DPC

Spalling
brickwork
and cracked
mortar joints

Gaps in and
around joinery

Cracks in rendering

Defective
vertical DPC

Figure 56   *Rain penetration*

Rain penetration

This is rain penetrating the external envelope either through the walls or the roof and appearing on the inside of the building as damp patches. After periods of heavy rain these patches will tend to spread and then dry out during prolonged periods of dry weather. They will, however, never completely disappear, as a moisture stain and in some cases even efflorescence (crystallized mineral salts) will be left on the surface. Mould growth (fungi resulting in dark-green or black patchy spots) may even occur in damp areas particularly behind furniture, in corners and other poorly ventilated locations. The main causes of rain penetration are shown in Figures 55 and 56. It can be seen that penetration takes place through gaps, cracks, holes and joints either in, around or between components and elements.

Roofs   Loose or missing tiles or slates including the hip and ridge capping tiles will allow rainwater to run down rafters, causing damp patches on the ceilings and tops of walls. These patches may appear some distance away from the defective area as the water spreads along timbers and across the ceiling etc. This dampness will also saturate any thermal insulation material making it ineffective. If left unrepaired, saturation of the roof timbers will occur leading to fungal decay in due course. Another major area of penetration is around the chimney stack and other roof-to-wall junctions; this may be due to cracked chimney pots, cracked or deteriorated flaunchings (the sloping mortar into which the pots are set), or corroded or pitted metal flashings (these cover the joint between the stack or wall and the roof); sometimes the flashings take the form of haunchings (a mortar fillet between the stack or wall and the roof) which may be cracked or deteriorated. Poor pointing to the stack can also be a cause of penetration. Any of these defects can cause large patches of damp on the internal walls.

Walls   Clearly rainwater travels downwards and when assisted by high winds it will travel sideways through gaps. But depending on the nature of the material, it can often move unassisted both sideways or upwards because of

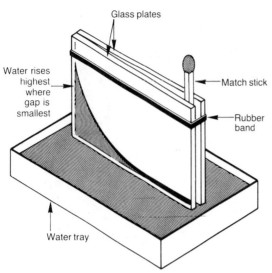

Figure 57   *Experiment to show capillarity*

capillary attraction (the phenomenon whereby water can travel against the force of gravity in fine spaces or between two surfaces which are close together; the smaller the space the greater the attraction. (See Figure 57.) There are two main conditions which promote capillarity in the external envelope. The fine cellular structure of some materials provides the interconnecting pores through which water can travel. Also the fine joints between components, e.g. wall and door or window frame, mortar joints between brickwork, close joints between overlapping components. The risk of capillarity is reduced or avoided by either:

physically separating the inside and outside surface by introducing an air space (e.g. cavity wall construction);

introducing a wide gap between components (e.g. anti-capillary grooves incorporated in window and external door frames; or

introducing a barrier to halt the water's travel (e.g. mastic pointing, DPCs, DPMs, moisture barriers and flashings etc.).

Over time, the water resistance of brick/stonework and their mortar joints will deterio-

rate. This deterioration can be accelerated by the action of frost. Rainwater may accumulate below the surface and freeze. Ice expands causing the brickwork/stonework and their mortar joints to *spall* (crumble away). The wall then offers little resistance to the weather and should be replaced. This entails either:

cutting the surface of the spalled components back and replacing with matching thin components (half bricks) finally repointing the whole wall; or

alternatively, the entire wall may be "hacked off" (cut back to remove spalling) and covered with one of the standard wall finishes, cement rendering, rough cast, pebble, ash, Tyrolean or silicone–nylon fibre.

Cracks in cement rendering and other wall finishes can be caused by shrinkage on drying, building movement or chemical attack. Once opened up, deterioration is accelerated by frost action. Small cracks may be enlarged and filled with a cement slurry. Large areas which may have 'blown' (come away) from the surface will require hacking back to sound (firmly adhering) work and replaced. With cavity wall construction, rainwater that does penetrate the outer leaf should simply run down inside the cavity and not reach the internal leaf. The vertical mortar joints of the outer leaf are sometimes raked out at intervals along the bottom of the cavity to provide weep holes through which the water can escape.

However when the cavity is bridged by a porous material (e.g. the collection of mortar droppings on wall ties during construction), the water will reach the inner leaf causing small isolated damp patches on the internal wall surface. The remedy for this fault is to remove one or two bricks of the outer leaf near the suspected bridge and either clean or replace the tie as necessary.

Dampness around door and window frames is likely to be caused by wind-assisted rain entering the joint between the wall and frame by the action of capillarity or by a defective vertical

DPC used around openings in cavity walls, where the inner and outer leaf join. An exterior mastic can be used to seal the joints but where DPCs are defective they will require cutting out and replacing. A check should be made at the sill level of frames. Cracked sills allow water to penetrate and therefore should be filled. The drip groove on the underside of the sill should be cleaned out as it often collects dirt/dust and is filled by repeated painting. The purpose of the drip groove is to break the under surface of the sill making the water drip off at this point and not run back underneath into the building.

Blocked or cracked gutters and down-pipes, dripping outside taps and constantly running overflows can cause an excessive concentration of water in one place which will be almost permanently damp. This will result in an accelerated deterioration of the wall and subsequent internal damp patches etc. The immediate fault can be easily rectified by repairing or replacing the defective component. But if left unattended the resulting damage to the building structure has most serious and costly implications.

Rising damp

This is normally moisture from below ground level rising and spreading up walls and through floors by capillarity. This most often occurs in older buildings. Many of these were built without DPCs and DPMs, or, where they were incorporated have broken down possibly with age (e.g. slate, a one time popular DPC material cracks with building movement, thus allowing capillarity). The visual result on the walls is a band of dampness and staining spreading up from the skirting level; wallpaper peeling from the surface and signs of efflorescence. The skirting, joists and floorboards adjacent to the missing or failed DPC are almost certain to be subjected to fungal attack. Solid floors may be almost permanently damp causing considerable damage to floor coverings and adjacent timber/furniture etc. Rising damp can still occur in buildings that have been equipped with DPCs and DPMs (see Figure 58). One of the main

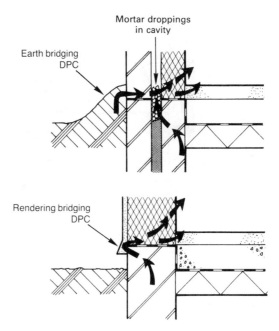

Figure 58 *Rising damp*

reasons for this is the bridging of DPCs; in the case of cavity walls, builders' mortar droppings or rubble may have collected at the bottom of the cavity, allowing moisture to rise above the DPC level; or earth in a flower bed being too high above the DPC; or a path/patio being laid too high above the DPC. (*Note*: DPCs are normally located at least two courses of brickwork (150 mm) above the adjacent ground level. This is because even very heavy rain is unlikely to bounce up and splash the walls much more than 100 mm from the surrounding surface. Thus the splashed rainwater is still prevented from rising above the DPC. Where the surrounding surface is later raised these splashes might bypass the DPC and result in rising damp. Weak porous rendering which has been continued over the DPC is another means by which the DPC may be bypassed.)

In solid floors with a DPM, rising damp can only occur if this is defective (see Figure 59). For example, it may have been penetrated by jagged hardcore during the pouring of the oversite or have been inadequately lapped (permitting capillarity between the lapped joint; or finally it

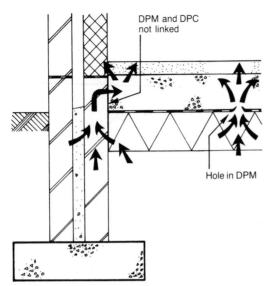

DPM and DPC not linked

Hole in DPM

Figure 59   *Rising damp*

may not have been linked in with the DPC in the surrounding walls (allowing moisture to bypass at this point).

The remedy to rising damp faults will of course vary; bridged or bypassed DPCs can be rectified by simply removing the cause, e.g. lowering the ground level or removing mortar and rubble from the cavity etc. Where the DPC itself is faulty or missing altogether, one can be inserted by either cutting out a few bricks at a time to allow the positioning of a new DPC or sawing away the mortar joint a section at a time and inserting one.

Alternatively, liquid silicone may be injected near the bottom of the wall. This soaks into the lower courses which then act as a moisture barrier preventing capillarity.

Localized faults in DPMs can be remedied by cutting out a section of the floor larger than the damp patch, down to the DPM, taking care not to cut through it. This should reveal the holed or badly lapped portion which can be repaired with a self-adhesive DPM. An alternative method which can also be used in floors without any DPM, is to cover the existing concrete floor with a liquid bituminous membrane or a sheet of

heavy-duty polythene sheeting before laying a new floor finish, although, to be effective it should be joined into the DPC.

Condensation

The results of this form of dampness are often mistakingly attributed to rain penetration or rising damp, as they can all cause damp patches, staining, mould growth, peeling wallpaper, efflorescence, the fungal attack of timber and generally damp, unhealthy living conditions. The water or moisture for condensation actually comes from within the building. People breathing, kettles boiling, food cooking, clothes washing and drying, bath water running etc. Each of these processes add more moisture to the air in the form of vapour.

Air is always capable of holding a certain amount of water vapour. The warmer the air, the more vapour it can hold, but when air cools the excess vapour will revert to water. This process is known as *condensation*. Thus whenever warm moist air meets a cool surface condensation will occur (see Figure 60). This can only be controlled effectively by achieving a proper balance between heating, ventilation and insulation. The building should be kept well heated but windows should be opened or mechanical ventilators used especially in kitch-

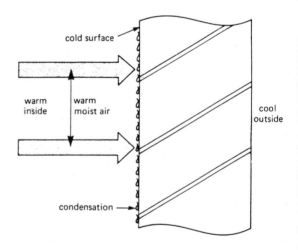

cold surface

warm inside

warm moist air

cool outside

condensation

Figure 60   *Surface condensation*

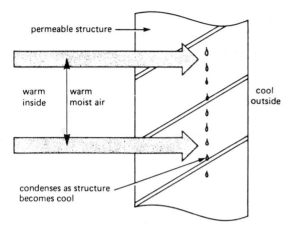

Figure 61 *Interstitial condensation.*

ens and bathrooms to allow the vapour-laden air escape outside and not spread through the building. External walls need thermally insulating to remove their cold surfaces. Both cavity wall insulation and lining the walls with a thin polystyrene veneer help a great deal. Double-glazed windows also help reduce condensation by preventing the warm moist air coming into direct contact with the cold outside pane of glass.

In addition to this surface condensation, there is another condensation problem which occurs when wall surfaces are warm. This is known as *interstitial* or *internal condensation*. This is illustrated in Figure 61. It is caused by the warm moist air passing into the permeable structure until it cools, at which point it condenses, thus leading to the same problems associated with penetrated and rising dampness.

Interstitial condensation can be dealt with either:

by the use of a vapour barrier (this prevents the passage of water vapour) on the warm inside of the wall, e.g. a polythene sheet or foilbacked plasterboard; or

by allowing this water vapour to pass through the structure into a cavity where it can be dispersed by ventilation.

Movement

The visual effects of movement (Figure 62) in buildings may apparently be of a minor nature, e.g. windows and doors that jamb or bind in their frames; fine cracks externally along mortar joints and rendering; fine cracks internally in plastered walls and along the ceiling line etc. They can however be the first signs of serious structural weakness. Movement in buildings takes two main forms these being: *ground movement* and *movement of materials*.

Ground movement

Any movement in the ground will cause settlement in the building. When it is slight and spread evenly over the building it may be acceptable, although when more than slight or is differential (more in one area than another), it can have serious consequences for the building's foundations and load-bearing members, requiring expensive temporary support (shoring) and subsequently, permanent underpinning (new foundations constructed under existing ones).

Ground movement is caused mainly by its expansion and shrinkage near the surface, owing

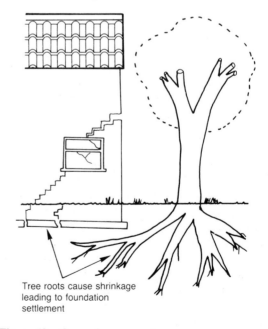

Tree roots cause shrinkage
leading to foundation
settlement

Figure 62 *Ground movement*

to wet and dry conditions. Compact granular ground suffers little movement, whereas clay ground is at high risk. Tree roots cause ground shrinkage owing to the considerable amounts of water they extract from it. Tree roots can extend out in all directions from its base, greater than its height. In addition, overloading of the structure beyond its original design load can also result in ground movement.

Frost also causes ground movement. Water in the ground on freezing expands. Where this is allowed to expand on the undersides of foundations it has a tendency to lift the building (known as *frost heave*) and drop it again on thawing. This repeated action often results in serious cracking. Freezing of ground water is limited in this country to about the top 600 mm in depth.

Movement in materials
All building materials will move to some extent owing to one or more of the following reasons: temperature changes, moisture-content changes and chemical changes. Provided the building is designed and constructed to accommodate these movements or steps are taken to prevent them, they should not lead to serious defects.

Temperature changes These cause expansion on heating and shrinkage on cooling; particularly affected are metals and plastics, although concrete, stonework, brickwork and timber can be affected also.

Moisture changes Many materials expand when wetted and shrink on drying. This is known as *moisture movement*. The greatest amount of moisture movement takes place in timber, which should be painted or treated to seal its surface. Brickwork, cement rendering and concrete can also be affected by moisture movement. Rapid drying of wetted brickwork in the hot sun can result in cracks, particularly around window and door openings.

Chemical changes These consist of the corrosion of metals and the sulphate attack of cement. Corrosion causes metals to expand and lose

strength. Corrosion of steel beams can lift brickwork causing cracks in the mortar joint. Bulges in cavity brickwork may be caused by corroded wall ties. The sulphate attack of cement is either in the ground or from products of combustion in chimneys. The sulphate mixes with water and causes cement to expand. Sulphate-Resisting Portland Cement (SRPC) should be used in conditions where high levels of sulphate are expected.

Chemical attack

Smoke containing chemicals is given off into the atmosphere as a result of many manufacturing processes; this mixes with water vapour and rainwater to form dilute or weak acid solutions. These solutions corrode iron and steel, break down paint films and erode the surfaces of brickwork, stonework and tiles. The useful life of materials in these environments can be prolonged by regular cleaning to remove the contamination. Exposure to sunlight can cause bleaching, colour fading of materials and even decomposition owing to solar radiation. Particularly affected are bituminous products, plastics and painted surfaces.

Biological attack

Timber, including structural, non-structural and timber-based manufactured items are the targets for biological attack. The agents of this are *fungi* and *wood-boring insects*. Given the right conditions an attack by one or both agents is almost inevitable.

Fungal attack
There are two main types of fungi that cause decay in building timbers, these being *dry rot* and *wet rot*.

Dry rot This is the more serious and is more difficult to eradicate than wet rot. It is caused by a fungus that feeds on the cellulose found mainly in sapwood (outer layers of a growing tree). This causes timber to lose strength and weight, develop cracks in brick-shape patterns,

Figure 63   *Timber after dry rot attack*

and finally to become so dry and powdery that it can easily be crumbled in the hand. The appearance of a piece of timber after an attack of dry rot is shown in Figure 63.

Two initial factors for an attack are damp timber in excess of about 20% moisture content (MC) and bad or non-existent ventilation.

Figure 64   *Advanced dry rot*

As the fungus is a living plant, an attack commences with the germination of its microscopic spores (seeds) that send out into the timber hyphae (roots) to feed on the cellulose. Once established, these hyphae branch out and spread through and over the timber forming a matt of cottonwool-like threads called mycelia. At this stage, the hyphae can penetrate plaster and brickwork in search of further timber supplies to feed on. This further timber supply need not be damp as the developed hyphae can conduct their own water supply, thus adjusting the moisture content as required. Finally the fruiting body, like a fleshy pancake with an orange brown centre, will start to ripen and eject into the air millions of the rust-red spores, to begin the process elsewhere. Very often in the early stages, apart from a damp musty mushroomy smell, there is little evidence of an attack. It is not until the wall panelling, skirting or floorboards are removed that the full effects are realized, as Figure 64 shows.

To eradicate an attack of dry rot, firstly rectify sources of dampness and bad ventilation;

Figure 65   *Wet rot in rafters*

remove all traces of decayed timber and at least 600 mm of apparently sound timber beyond the last signs of attack; burn all affected timber including swept-up dust, dirt and old wood shavings etc. (this prevents spreading and kills the hyphae and spores); strip plaster from walls, wire brush brickwork, heat up brickwork with a blow lamp to sterilize, and brush or spray wall with a dry-rot fungicide (this kills any hyphae and spores in the walls). Finally work may be reinstated with preservative treated timber. (*Note:* The idea behind preservative treatment is to poison the food supply of fungi and wood-boring insects, by applying a toxic liquid to the timber.)

Wet rot   This is also caused by a fungus, but it does not normally involve such drastic eradication treatment, as it does not spread to the same extent as dry rot. It feeds on wet timber (30% to 50% MC) and most often found in cellars, neglected external joinery, ends of rafters, under leaking sinks or baths and under impervious (waterproof) floor coverings. During an attack, the timber becomes soft, darkens to a blackish colour and develops cracks along the grain. Very often timber decays internally with a fairly thin skin of apparently sound timber remaining on the surface. The hyphae when apparent are dark brown or black; internally hyphae may be white and form into sheets. Its fruiting body, which is rarely found, is of an irregular shape and normally olive green in colour, as are the spores. Figure 65 shows the appearance after an attack of wet rot in the rafters of a roof.

To eradicate an attack of wet rot   all that is normally required is to cure the source of wetness and allow the timber to dry out. Replacement of soft timber may be required after an extensive attack particularly where structural timber is concerned.

Wood-boring insects
This is also known as woodworm after the larvae which are able to feed on, and digest, the substance of wood. The majority of the damage done to building timber in the UK can be attributed to five species in Table 5 which includes their identifying characteristics.

The female adult beetle lays eggs during the summer months, usually in the end grain, open joints, or cracks in the timber. This affords the eggs a certain amount of protection until the larvae hatch. The larvae then start their damaging journey by boring into the timber, consuming it and then excreting it as a fine dust. This stage varies between six months and ten years depending on the species. During the early spring, at the close of this stage, the larvae bore out a pupal chamber near the timber surface, where they undergo the transformation into adult beetles. This takes a short period after which the beetles bite out of the timber leaving characteristic flight holes. The presence of flight holes is often the first external sign of an attack.

Table 5 **Wood-boring insects**

Name	Actual size	Location and timber attacked
Furniture beetle	beetle flight holes	Softwoods and the sapwood of hardwood; causes considerable damage to timber, flooring and furniture
Death-watch beetle		Mainly hardwoods in old damp buildings (churches); often in association with fungal attack
Lyctus beetle (powder post)		Sapwood of freshly-cut hardwoods; normally in timber yards before use
House long-horn beetle		Sapwood of softwoods; mainly roof timbers
Weevils		Damp or decayed hardwoods and softwoods; often found around sinks, baths, toilets and in cellars

After emerging from the timber the beetles' instinct is to mate, lay eggs and then die, thus completing one life cycle and starting another.

To eradicate an attack of wood-boring insects open up the affected area (take up floorboards etc.), remove and burn badly affected timber and replace with new preservative-treated timber. Brush timber to remove dust, strip off surface coating, e.g. paint, varnish etc. (woodworm fluid will not penetrate surface coatings).

Apply two coats of a proprietary woodworm killer by brush or spray to all timber, even apparently unaffected timber. Pay particular attention to cracks, joints, end grain and flight holes. Inspections for fresh flight holes should be carried out for several successive summers. A further treatment of fluid will be required if any are found (fresh bore dust around the affected area indicates fresh flight holes).

Self-assessment questions

1 Define the term "building maintenance"

_____

_____

_____

_____

2 Name *two* factors that affect the rate and extent to which a building deteriorates

_____

_____

_____

_____

3 Name *three* agents to which deterioration in buildings can be directly attributed

_____

_____

_____

_____

4 Produce a sketch to show *two* methods by which moisture may bypass DPCs

5 Define the term "capillary attraction"

_____

_____

_____

_____

6 Name *two* causes of movement in buildings and identify their likely effect

_____

_____

_____

_____

7 State the purpose of treating
timber with preservative

  _____

  _____

  _____

  _____

8 Identify *two* causes of rising
damp and suggest a remedy
for each

  _____

  _____

  _____

  _____

9 List *two* defects under each of
the following headings that
can lead to the rapid de-
terioration of a building: (i)
movement; (ii) biological
attack

  _____

  _____

  _____

10 Identify the probable causes
of the following defects:
(i) small isolated damp
patches at intervals on
the internal leaf of an
external cavity wall;
(ii) small holes in the surface
of timber with fine dust
around them;
(iii) damp patch in the centre
of a solid ground floor

  _____

  _____

  _____

  _____

  _____

  _____

Assignment one

Approximately three hours are required to answer this assignment

Assignments are intended to illustrate some of the day-to-day problems/enquiries which you as a member of the building industry may encounter.

For the purposes of this assignment you are to assume that you are one-half of a couple that wish to set up a home together. After having extensively toured estate agents looking for suitable properties, you have chosen to make an offer of purchase for the building (shown in Figures 66 and 67) which was built in 1965.

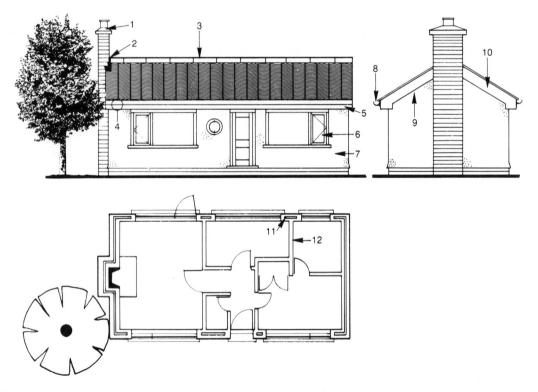

Figure 66   *Plan and elevations*

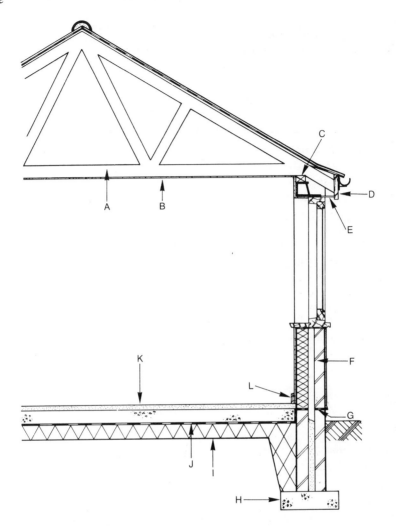

Figure 67   *Section*

You should attempt all six tasks of this assignment, which are based on this building. Illustrate your answers with sketches where appropriate.

Task one

1 State the type, category and
  style of the accommodation _____

_____

_____

_____

2 Name and describe the type
  of structure

_____

_____

_____

_____

Task two

3 Define the following terms
  and indicate an example of
  each of them on the section
  shown in Figure 67: (i) substructure; (ii) superstructure;
  (iii) primary element; (iv)
  secondary element; (v)
  finishing element; (vi) component

_____

_____

_____

_____

_____

Task three

4 Name the type of foundations
  illustrated

_____

_____

_____

_____

5 State *three* factors that affect
  the depth of foundations

_____

_____

_____

_____

6 Sketch an alternative type of
  ground-floor construction

Task four

7 Using the following items,
  identify the numbered features shown in Figure 66; not

_____

_____

all of the items are applicable: Gable, ridge, sash, hip, verge, eaves, parapet, cavity, partition wall, cladding, lintel, flashing, casement, barge board, fascia board, gutter, rendering, casement, flaunching.

8 Identify the lettered elements/components shown in the section (Figure 67), name the material indicated, and where appropriate state a suitable alternative

Task five

9 At the time the building was constructed there was little consideration given to thermal insulation. Suggest *three* ways of improving this to modern standards

10 During a close inspection of the building you notice the following defects. State for each a possible cause and remedy

 (i) Small damp patch in the centre of lounge floor
 (ii) Rafters next to chimney stack are wet and show signs of fungal attack
 (iii) Vertical cracks in walls down the side of chimney and under lounge window

Task six

11 Write a letter to the building owner making a reduced offer of purchase. Justify your reduction in the price by the costs involved in improving the thermal insulation and rectifying the defects

The Process of Building and the Building Team

After working through this part of the book the student should be able to:

1 Specify the stages in designing a building, from defining function to production of working drawings.

2 State the role of each of the main members of the design and construction team.

3 Indicate the main requirements for establishing and maintaining good working relationships within the construction team.

4 State the structure of contracting firms of various sizes and of the roles and responsibilities of employers and employees.

5 State the main principles of organization and management of jobs.

6 State the main stages in the construction of buildings.

7 Outline the general requirements for safety and welfare in construction work.

Topic 8
The building team

The construction of a building is a complex process, which requires a team of professionals working together to produce the desired results. This team of professionals which is collectively known as the **building team** is a combination of the following parties:

1 Client
2 Architect
3 Quantitiy surveyor
4 Specialist engineers
5 Clerk of works
6 Local authority
7 Health and safety inspector
8 Building contractors
9 Sub-contractors
10 Suppliers

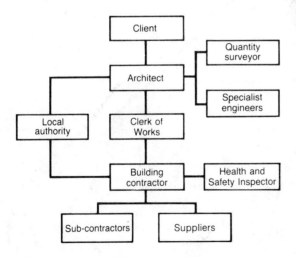

Figure 68 *The building team*

There is a recognized pattern by which the building team operates and communicates. This is illustrated in the form of a line diagram in Figure 68.

The client

This is the person or persons who have an actual need for building work, e.g. the construction of a new house, office block, factory or extensions, repairs and alterations to existing buildings. The client is the most important member of the building team, for without whom the work would simply not exist. He is responsible for the over-all financing of the work and in effect employs either directly or indirectly the entire team. Clients can vary in size from a single person to a very large organization. For example:

Private individual
Association
Partnership
Public company
Local authority
Nationalized industry
Statutory undertaking
Government department

The architect

The architect is the client's agent and is considered to be the leader of the building team. The role of an architect is to interpret the client's requirements, translate them into a building form and generally supervise all aspects of the work until it is completed. All architects must be registered with the Architects' Registration Council, the majority of them also being members of the Royal Institute of British Architects using the designatory letters RIBA.

The quantity surveyor

In effect, the quantity surveyor or QS as they are often termed is the client's building economic consultant or accountant. This specialist surveyor advises during the design stage as to how the building may be constructed within the client's budget, and measures the quantity of labour and materials necessary to complete the building work from drawings and other information prepared and supplied by the architect. These quantities are incorporated into a document known as the *Bill of Quantities* which is used by building contractors when pricing the building work. During the contract, the quantity surveyor will measure and prepare valuations of the work carried out up to date to enable interim payments to be made to the building contractor and at the end of the building contract will prepare the final account for presentation to the client. In addition, the quantity surveyor will advise the architect on the cost of additional works or variations.

The specialist engineers

These are engaged as part of the design team to assist the architect in the design of the building within their specialist fields, e.g.

Civil engineers
Structural engineers
Service engineers

They will prepare drawings and calculations to enable specialist contractors to quote for these areas of work. In addition, during the contract the specialist engineers will make regular inspections to ensure the installation is carried out in accordance with the design.

The clerk of works

Appointed by the architect/client to act as their on-site representative. On large contracts s/he will be resident on-site whilst on smaller ones will only visit periodically. The clerk of works or COW is an 'inspector of works' and as such will ensure that the contractor carries out the work in accordance with the drawings and other contract documents. This includes inspecting both the standard of workmanship and the quality of materials. The COW will make regular reports back to the architect, keep a diary in case of disputes, make a daily record of the weather, and of personnel employed on-site and any stoppages. S/he also agrees general matters directly with the building contractor although these must be confirmed by the architect to be valid.

The local authority

The local authority normally has the responsibility of ensuring that proposed building works conform to the requirements of relevant planning and building legislation. For this purpose, they employ *planning officers* and *building control officers* to approve and inspect building work. In some areas, building control officers are known as *building inspectors* or *district surveyors* (DS).

The health and safety inspector

The health and safety inspector (also known as the *factory inspector*) is employed by the Health and Safety Executive. It is the inspector's duty to ensure that the government legislation concerning health and safety is fully implemented by the building contractor.

The building contractor

The building contractor enters into a contract with the client to carry out, in accordance with the contract documents, certain building works. Each contractor will develop his/her own

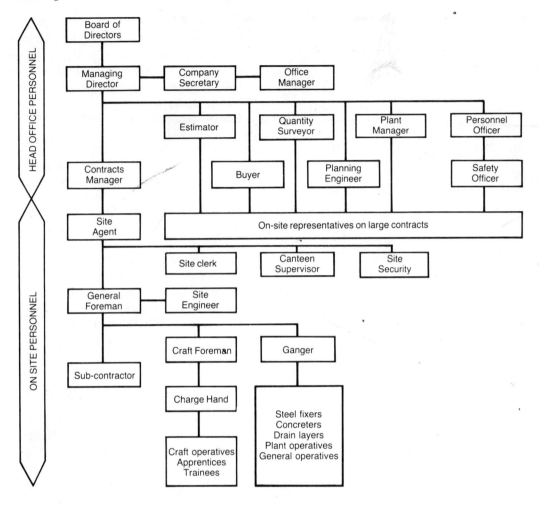

Figure 69 *The organization structure of building contractors*

method and procedures for tendering and carrying out building work which in turn, together with the size of the contract, will determine the personnel required. It is necessary, in order to function effectively, for contractors to establish and maintain good working relationships within their construction team/organization. This can be achieved by good cooperation and communication between the various sections; good working conditions, e.g. pay, holidays, status, security, future opportunities and a pleasant, safe working environment; and finally by nurturing a good team spirit where people are motivated, rewarded for their successes and allowed to work on their own initiative under supervision for the good of the company as a whole. Figure 69 shows in line diagram form a typical contractor's head office and site organization structure.

The estimators
Their role is to arrive at an overall cost for carrying out a building contract. In order to arrive at the overall cost, they will break down each item contained in the Bill of Quantities into its constituent parts (labour, materials and

plant) and apply a rate to each, representing the amount it will cost the contractor to complete the item. Added to the total cost of all the items will be a percentage for overheads (head/site office costs, site management/administration salaries) and profit.

The buyer

As the title suggests, the buyers are responsible for the purchase of materials. They will obtain quotations, negotiate the best possible terms, order the materials and ensure that they arrive on-site at the required time, in the required quantity and quality.

The building contractor's quantity surveyor

This is the building contractor's building economist. S/he will measure and evaluate the building work carried out each month including the work of any subcontractors. An interim valuation is prepared by him/her on the basis of these measurements and passed on to the client for payment. S/he is also responsible for preparing interim costings to see whether or not the contract is within budget; finally s/he will prepare and agree the final accounts on completion of the contract.

The planning engineer

S/he is responsible for the pre-contract planning of the building project. It is his/her role to plan the work in such a way as to ensure the most efficient/economical use of labour, materials, plant and equipment. Within their specialist field of work, the planning engineers are often supported by a *work study engineer* (to examine various building operations to increase productivity) and a *bonus surveyor* (to operate an incentive scheme which is also aimed at increasing productivity by awarding operatives additional money for work completed over a basic target).

The plant manager

S/he is responsible for all items of mechanical plant (machines and power tools) used by the building contractor. S/he at the request of the contracts manager/site agent will supply from stock, purchase or hire, the most suitable plant item to carry out a specific task. The plant manager is also responsible for the maintenance of plant items and the training of operatives who use them.

The safety officer

S/he is responsible to senior management for all aspects of health and safety. The role is to advise on all health and safety matters; carry out safety inspections; keep safety records; investigate accidents; and finally arrange staff safety training.

Note: Each of these previously mentioned head-office personnel is the leader of a specialist service section and depending on the size of the firm will employ one or more technicians for assistance. On very large contracts they may also have a representative resident on-site.

The contract's manager

This is the supervisor of the site management teams, on a number of contracts. The contract's manager has an overall responsibility for planning, management and building operations. S/he will liaise between the head office staff and the site agents on the contracts for which they are responsible.

The site agent

Also known as the *site manager* or *project manager*, the site agent is the building contractor's resident on-site representative and leader of the site work force. S/he is directly responsible to the contracts manager for the day-to-day planning, management and building operations.

The general foreman

S/he works under the site agent and is responsible for coordinating the work of the craft foreman, ganger and subcontractors. S/he will also advise the site agent on constructional problems; liaise with the clerk of works; and may also be responsible for the day-to-day employing and dismissing of operatives, although this role is often coordinated by the head office personnel officer who, amongst other things, is responsible for changes in the work force strength.

The site engineer

The site engineers or *surveyors* as they are sometimes called, work alongside the general foreman. They are responsible for ensuring that the building is the correct size and in the right place. They will set out and check the line, level and verticality (plumb) of the building during its construction.

The craft foreman

S/he works under the general foreman to organize and supervise the work of a specific craft, e.g. foreman bricklayer and foreman carpenter.

The ganger

Like the craft foreman, the ganger also works under the general foreman but this time s/he is responsible for the organization and supervision of the general building operatives.

The chargehand

On large contracts employing a large number of craftsmen in each craft (normally bricklayers and carpenters) chargehands are often appointed to assist the craft foreman and supervise a sub-section of the work. For example, a foreman carpenter may have charge-hands to supervise the carcassing team (floor joists and roofs); the first fixing team (flooring, frames and studwork); the second fixing team (doors, skirting, architraves and joinery fitments). Chargehands are often known as *working foremen* because, in addition to supervising their small team, they also carry out the skilled physical work of their craft.

The operative

This is the name given to the person who carries out the actual physical building work. Operatives can be divided into *two* main groups:

Craft operatives

These are the skilled craftsman who perform specialist tasks with a range of materials, e.g. bricklayer, carpenter, electrician, painter, plasterer and plumber.

Building operatives

These are further subdivided into:

General building operatives who mix concrete, lay drains, off-load material and assist craft operatives; and

Specialist building operatives, e.g. ceiling fixer, glazer, plant mechanic and scaffolder.

The site clerk

This person is responsible for all site administrative duties and the control of materials on-site. S/he will record the arrival and departure of all site personnel; prepare wage sheets for head office; record the delivery and transfer of plant items; record and check delivery of materials and note their ultimate distribution (assisted by a storekeeper).

The sub-contractors

The building contractor may call upon a specialist firm to carry out a specific part of the building work; for this they will enter into a sub-contract, hence the term sub-contractor. Building contractors generally sub-contract work such as structural steelwork, formwork, mechanical services, electrical installations, plastering, tiling and often painting. However, at certain times they may also sub-contract the major crafts of bricklaying and carpentry. Sub-contractors may be labour-only (where they contract to fit the building contractor's material), or they may contract to supply and fix their own material. Architects can name or nominate a specific sub-contractor in the contract documents and this sub-contractor must be used. They are then known as *nominated sub-contractors.*

The suppliers ✓

Building materials, equipment and plant are supplied by a wide range of merchants, manufacturers and hirers. The building contractor will negotiate with these to supply their goods in the required quantity and quality, at the agreed price, and finally in accordance with the building contractor's delivery requirements. Architects may nominate specific suppliers who must be used and are therefore termed *nominated suppliers*.

Self-assessment questions

Question	*Your answer*
1 Name the *ten* members that form the building team	
2 Describe the role of *four* of those given in your answer to Question 1	
3 Use a simple line diagram to show a typical on-site organization structure	
4 Identify the personnel who are associated with the following abbreviations: (i) RIBA; (ii) QS; (iii) COW; (iv) DS	
5 Name the person who is responsible on-site for the day-to-day planning, management and building operations	

6 Explain the word 'nominated' when applied to material suppliers

_____

_____

_____

_____

7 Explain briefly how building contractors may achieve and maintain, good working relationships within their organizations

_____

_____

_____

_____

8 A specification for building works is normally prepared for a client by the:
   (a) building control officer
   (b) clerk of works
   (c) estimator
   (d) quantity surveyor?

   a   b   c   d

The design process

The design of a building is usually in the hands of a team of specialists brought together for this specific purpose. This design team, all of whom are employed directly by the client, will consist of the:

(i) Client (or specialist advisor)
(ii) Architect (leader)
(iii) Quantity surveyor (economic consultant)
(iv) Specialist engineers (specialist consultants)

In addition, depending on the nature of the work, it may also include the:

(v) Interior designer
(vi) Landscape designer
(vii) Town planner

The first step in building projects is for a prospective building client to appoint an architect to act for him/her in the construction or alteration of a building. On being appointed, the architect will obtain from the client a *brief*, consisting of full details of his/her requirements and the proposed site. In the brief, the client will define requirements with regards to the building's size, intended usage, style/design and finally the maximum expenditure. Having inspected the site and assessed the feasibility of the client's requirements, the architect will prepare sketch designs, submit them to the client for approval and apply for outline planning permission.

When approval is obtained, the design team is formed to consider the brief and sketch designs, and come up with proposals that will form the basis of the structure. Location drawings, outline specifications and preliminary details of costs are then produced and submitted to the client for approval. If these details are acceptable, applications will be made for full planning permission and building regulations approval (if applicable). While this is taking place, contract documents will be prepared and sent to a number of building contractors for them to produce and submit tenders.

The returned tenders will be considered by the quantity surveyor who will advise the architect and client of the most suitable contractor. The client and contractor will then sign the contract.

Contract documents

These documents will vary depending on the nature of the work, but will normally consist of:

Working drawings
Specification
Schedules
Bill of Quantities
Conditions of contract

Working drawings

These are scale drawings showing the plans, elevations, sections, details and locality of the proposed construction. These drawings can be divided into a number of main types:

Location drawings (Figure 70)

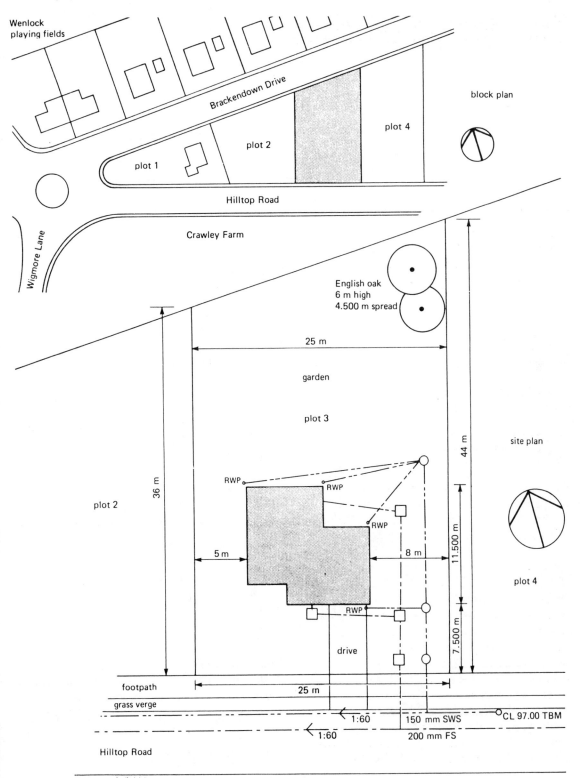

Figure 70   *Location drawings*

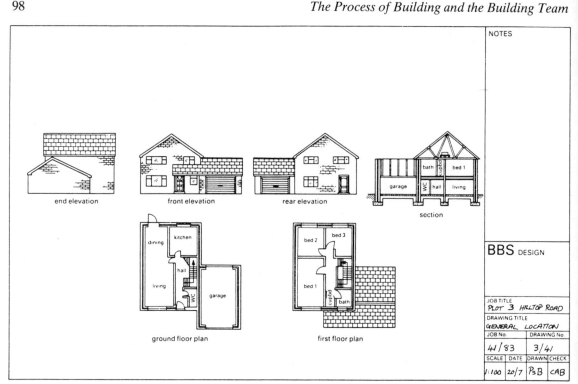

Figure 71   *General location plans*

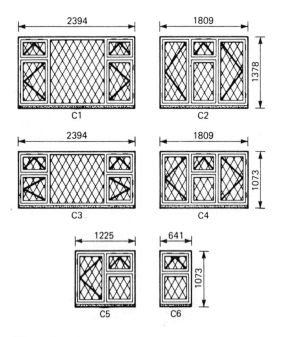

Figure 72   *Component range drawing*

Block plans, scale 1:2500, 1:1250, identify the proposed site in relation to the surrounding area.

Site plans, scale 1:500, 1:200, give the position of the proposed building and the general layout of roads, services and drainage etc. on the site.

General location plans (Figure 71), scale 1:200, 1:100, 1:50, show the position occupied by the various areas within the building and identify the location of the principal elements and components.

Component drawings

Range drawings (Figure 72), scale 1:100, 1:50, 1:20, show the basic sizes and reference system of a standard range of components.

Detail drawings (Figure 73), scale 1:10, 1:5, 1:1, show all the information that is required in order to manufacture a particular component.

Figure 73 *Component detail drawing*

serving hatch   vertical section

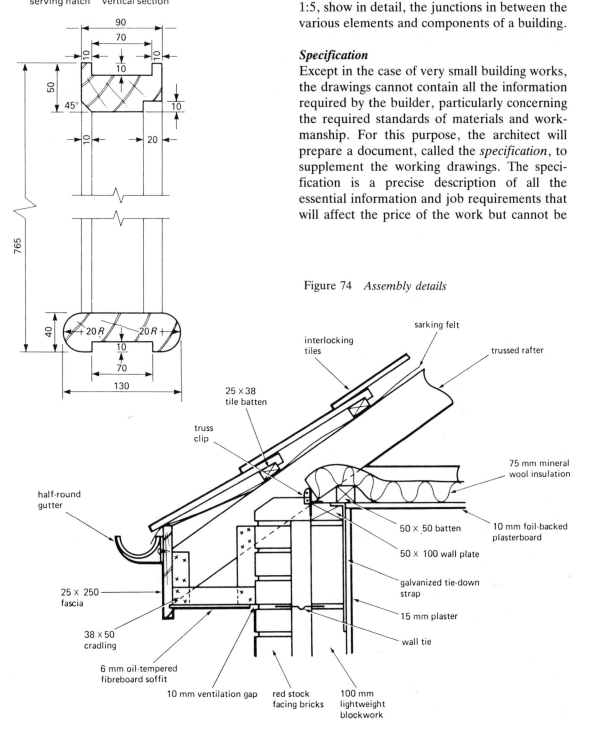

Assembly drawings
Assembly details (Figure 74), scale 1:20, 1:10, 1:5, show in detail, the junctions in between the various elements and components of a building.

Specification
Except in the case of very small building works, the drawings cannot contain all the information required by the builder, particularly concerning the required standards of materials and workmanship. For this purpose, the architect will prepare a document, called the *specification*, to supplement the working drawings. The specification is a precise description of all the essential information and job requirements that will affect the price of the work but cannot be

Figure 74   *Assembly details*

shown on the drawings. Typical items included in the specification are:

Site description

Restrictions (limited access and working hours etc.)

Availability of services (water, electricity, gas, telephone)

Description of materials, quality, size, tolerance, and finish

Description of workmanship, quality, fixing and jointing

Other requirements: site clearance, making good on completion, nominated suppliers and sub-contractors, who passes the work etc.

Various clauses of a typical specification are shown in Figure 75.

Schedules

These are used to record repetitive design information about a range of similar components. The main areas where schedules are used include: Doors, frames, linings; windows; ironmongery; joinery fitments; sanitary ware; heating units, radiators; finishes, floor, wall and ceiling; lintels; and steel reinforcement.

The information that schedules contain is essential when preparing estimates and tenders. In addition, schedules are also extremely useful when measuring quantities, locating work and checking deliveries of materials and components.

Obtaining information from a schedule about any particular item is fairly straightforward. For example, the range drawing, floor plans and door schedules shown in Figures 76, 77, and 78 are consulted. Details relevant to a particular door opening are indicated in the schedules by a dot or cross; a figure is also included where more than one item is required.) The following information concerning the WC door D2 has been extracted or 'taken off' from the schedules:

One polished plywood internal flush door type B2 762 mm × 1981 mm × 35 mm hung on 38 mm × 125 mm softwood lining with planted stops, transom and 6 mm obscure tempered safety-glass fanlight infill, including the following ironmongery:

One pair of 75 mm brass butts
One mortise lock-latch
One brass mortise lock/latch furniture
Two brass coat hooks

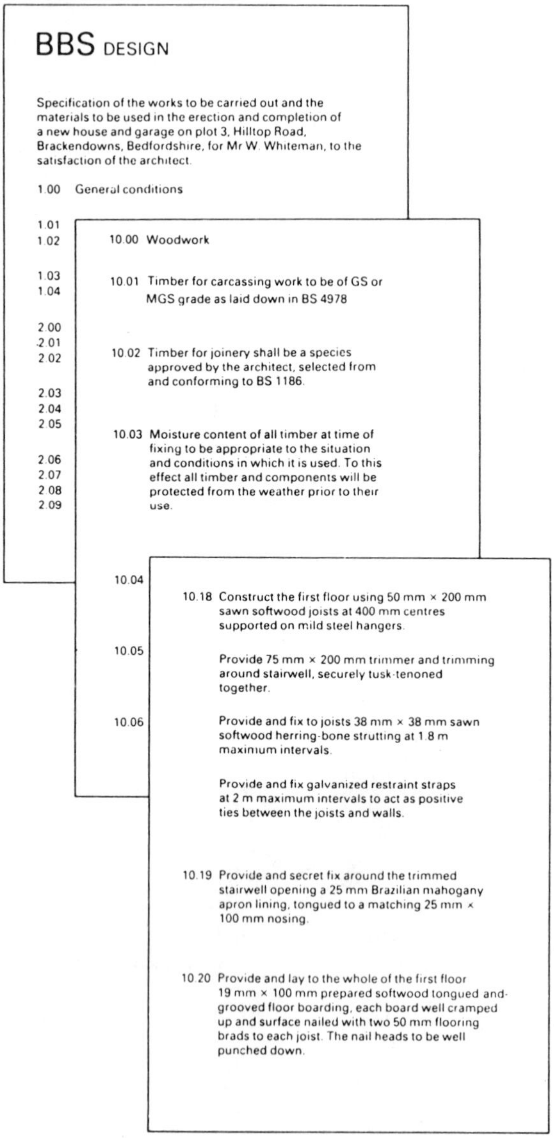
BBS DESIGN

Specification of the works to be carried out and the materials to be used in the erection and completion of a new house and garage on plot 3, Hilltop Road, Brackendowns, Bedfordshire, for Mr W. Whiteman, to the satisfaction of the architect.

1.00 General conditions

1.01
1.02
1.03
1.04
2.00
2.01
2.02
2.03
2.04
2.05
2.06
2.07
2.08
2.09

10.00 Woodwork

10.01 Timber for carcassing work to be of GS or MGS grade as laid down in BS 4978

10.02 Timber for joinery shall be a species approved by the architect, selected from and conforming to BS 1186.

10.03 Moisture content of all timber at time of fixing to be appropriate to the situation and conditions in which it is used. To this effect all timber and components will be protected from the weather prior to their use.

10.04
10.05
10.06

10.18 Construct the first floor using 50 mm × 200 mm sawn softwood joists at 400 mm centres supported on mild steel hangers.

Provide 75 mm × 200 mm trimmer and trimming around stairwell, securely tusk-tenoned together.

Provide and fix to joists 38 mm × 38 mm sawn softwood herring-bone strutting at 1.8 m maximum intervals.

Provide and fix galvanized restraint straps at 2 m maximum intervals to act as positive ties between the joists and walls.

10.19 Provide and secret fix around the trimmed stairwell opening a 25 mm Brazilian mahogany apron lining, tongued to a matching 25 mm × 100 mm nosing.

10.20 Provide and lay to the whole of the first floor 19 mm × 100 mm prepared softwood tongued-and-grooved floor boarding, each board well cramped up and surface nailed with two 50 mm flooring brads to each joist. The nail heads to be well punched down.

Figure 75 *Extracts from a specification*

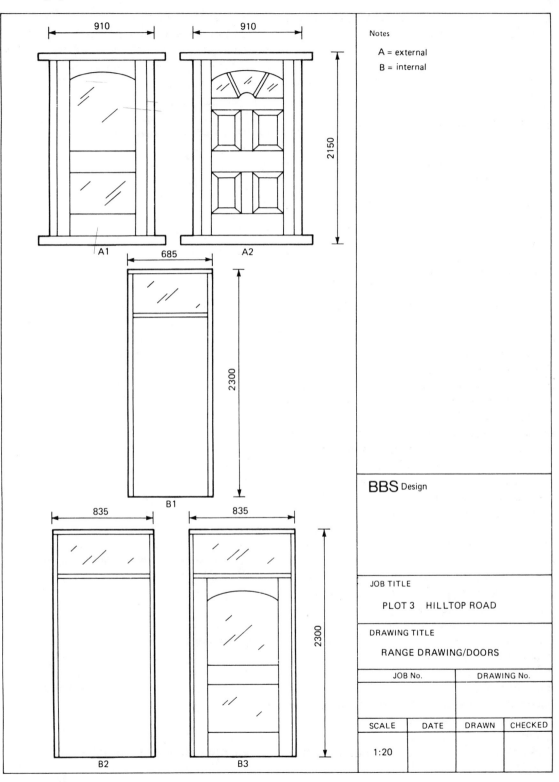

Figure 76   *Door range drawing*

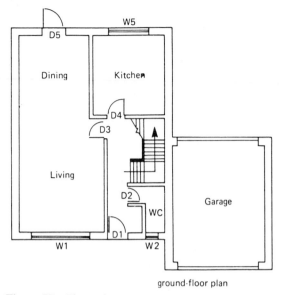

ground-floor plan   first-floor plan

Figure 77   *Floor plans*

Bill of Quantities

The Bill of Quantities (BoQ) is prepared by the quantity surveyor. This document gives a complete description and measure of the quantities of labour, material and other items required to carry out the work, based on drawings, specification and schedules. Its use ensures that all estimators prepare their tender on the same information. An added advantage is that as each individual item is priced in the tender, they can be used for valuing the work in progress and also form the basis for valuing any variation to the contract.

All bills of quantities will contain the following information:

Preliminaries

These deal with the general particulars of the work, such as the names of the parties involved, details of the works, description of the site and conditions of the contract etc.

Preambles

These are introductory clauses to each trade covering descriptions of the material and workmanship similar to those stated in the specifications.

Measured quantities

A description and measurement of an item of work, the measurement being given in metres run, metres square, kilograms etc. or just enumerated as appropriate.

Provisional quantities

Where an item cannot be measured accurately, an approximate quantity to be allowed for can be stated. Adjustments will be made when the full extent of the work is known.

Prime cost sum (PC sum)

This is an amount of money to be included in the tender for work services or materials provided by a nominated sub-contractor, supplier or statutory body.

Provisional sum

A sum of money to be included in the tender for work which has not yet been finally detailed or for a 'contingency sum' to cover the cost of any unforeseen work. Extracts from a typical Bill of Quantities are shown in Figure 79.

Standard method of measurement

In order to ensure that the Bill of Quantities is

Description	D1	D2	D3	D4	D5	D6	D7	D8	D9	D10			NOTES
Type (see range)													
External glazed A1					●								
External panelled A2	●												
Internal flush B1								●					
Internal flush B2		●				●	●	●		●			
Internal glazed B3			●	●									
Size													
813 mm ⁄ 2032 mm × 44 mm	●				●								
762 mm × 1981 mm × 35 mm		●	●	●		●	●	●		●			
610 mm × 1981 mm × 35 mm								●					
Material													**BBS** DESIGN
Hardwood	●												
Softwood			●	●	●								
Plywood/polished		●											JOB TITLE
Plywood/painted						●	●	●	●	●			PLOT 3 Hilltop Road
Infill													DRAWING TITLE
6 mm tempered safety glass													Door Schedule/doors
clear			●	●	●								JOB NO. DRAWING NO.
obscured	●												
													SCALE DATE DRAWN CHECKED

Description	D1	D2	D3	D4	D5	D6	D7	D8	D9	D10			NOTES
Frames													
75 mm × 100 mm (outward opening)					●								
75 mm × 100 mm (inward opening)	●												
Linings													
38 mm × 125 mm		●	●	●									
38 mm × 100 mm						●	●	●	●	●			
Shape													
Rebated stop	●				●								
Planted stop		●	●	●		●	●	●	●	●			
Transom		●	●	●		●	●	●	●	●			
Sill	●				●								**BBS** DESIGN
Material													
Hardwood	●												
Softwood		●	●	●	●	●	●	●	●	●			JOB TITLE
Fanlight infill													PLOT 3 Hilltop Road
6 mm tempered safety glass													DRAWING TITLE
clear													Door Schedule/frames/lining
obscured		●							●				JOB NO. DRAWING NO.
6 mm plywood								●					SCALE DATE DRAWN CHECKED

Figure 78 *Door schedules*

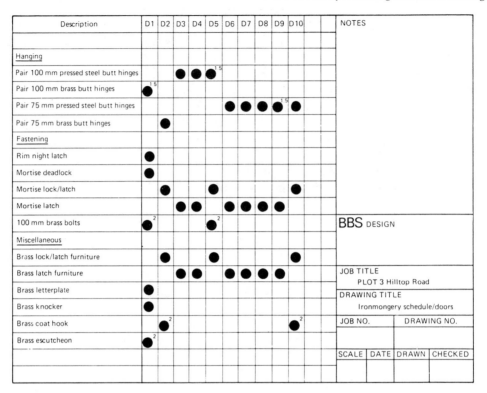

Figure 78 *continued*

readily understood and interpreted in a consistent manner by all concerned, the various items should be described and measured in accordance with the latest edition of *The Standard Method of Measurement of Building Works* (SMM). This document, prepared by the Royal Institution of Chartered Surveyors and The Building Employers' Confederation (BEC), provides a uniform basis for measuring building work and it embodies the essentials of good practice.

Conditions of contract

Most building work is carried out under a 'standard form of contract' such as the Joint Contractors Tribunal (JCT) forms of contract or the BEC form of contract. The actual standard form of contract used will depend on the following:

Type of client (local authority, public limited company or private individual);

size and type of work (sub-contract, small or major project, package deal);

contract documents (with or without quantities or approximate quantities).

A building contract is basically a legal agreement between the parties involved, in which the contractor agrees to carry out the building work and the client agrees to pay a sum of money for the work. The contract should also include the rights and obligations of all parties and details of procedures for variations, interim payments' retention and the defects liability period. These terms can be defined as follows:

Variation

This is a modification of the specification by the client or architect. The contractor must be issued with a written variation order or architect's instruction. Any cost adjustment as a

ITEM	DESCRIPTION	QUANTITY	UNIT	RATE	AMOUNT
	Preliminaries				
	Name of parties				
	Client				£
	Mr W. Whiteman				
	Whiteman Enterprises				
	Engineering House				
	Bedford				
	Architect BBS Design				

ITEM	DESCRIPTION	QUANTITY	UNIT	RATE	AMOUNT
	Preambles				
	woodwork (cont.)				£
A	Impregnated timber is timber which has been pressure impregnated with an approved preservative by a specialist firm. Any timber cut on the site after treatment must have a liberal brush application of the same preservative in accordance with the manufacturer's instructions.				

ITEM	DESCRIPTION	QUANTITY	UNIT	RATE	AMOUNT
	Super structure (upper floor)				
	Woodwork				£
	Impregnated sawn softwood				
A	50 mm × 200 mm joist	85	M		
B	75 mm × 200 mm joist	7	M		

ITEM	DESCRIPTION	QUANTITY	UNIT	RATE	AMOUNT
	Internal doors (cont.)				£
	Ironmongery				
	Supply and fix the following ironmongery as described with matching screws to softwood or plywood faced doors.				
	Note: references refer to BBS catalogue no. 6b				
A	*Pair* 100 mm pressed steel butt hinges (1.47)	2	No		
B	*Pair* 75 mm pressed steel butt hinges (1.48)	4.5	No		
C	*Pair* 75 mm brass butt hinges (1.23)	1	No		
D	Mortise lock/latch (2.14)	2	No		
E	Mortise latch (2.15)	6	No		
F	Mortise lock/latch furniture (3.14)	2	No		
G	Mortise latch furniture (3.15)	6	No		
H	Coat hook (6.25)	2	No		
J	Provide the P.C. sum of *three hundred and fifty pounds* £350 for the supply and installation by a specialist subcontractor of two overhead garage doors.				350 00
K	*Add* for expenses and profit.			%	
L	Include the provisional sum of *one hundred and fifty pounds* £150 for contingencies.				150 00
	Carried to Collection			£	

Figure 79 *Extracts from a bill of quantities*

result of the variation must be agreed between the quantity surveyor and the contractor.

Interim payment

This is a monthly or periodic payment made to the contractor by the client. It is based on the quantity surveyor's interim valuation of the work done and the materials purchased by the contractor. On agreeing the interim valuation, the architect will issue an *interim certificate* which authorizes the client to make the payment.

Final account

This is the final payment on completion. The architect will issue a *certificate of practical completion* when the building work is finished. The quantity surveyor and the contractor will then agree the final account less the retention.

Retention

This is a sum of money which is retained by the client until the end of an agreed *defects liability period*.

Defects liability period

This is a period normally of six months after practical completion to allow any defect to become apparent. The contractor will be entitled to the retention after any defects have been rectified to the architect's satisfaction.

Self-assessment questions

Questions   *Your answer*

1 Name and describe the role of the design team's leader

_____

_____

_____

_____

2 Name the design team's economic consultant

_____

_____

_____

_____

3 List the main contract documents

_____

_____

_____

_____

4 Distinguish between 'measured quantities' and 'provisional quantities'

_____

_____

_____

_____

5 Explain what is meant by the
  term 'defects liability period'

_____

_____

_____

_____

6 Describe the purpose of *The
  Standard Method of Measurement of Building Works*

_____

_____

_____

_____

Topic 10
The construction process

The construction stage in the total building process can itself be sub-divided into two stages:

The pre-construction stage

This involves tendering and contract planning.

The on-site construction stage

This consists of the actual physical tasks and the administration processes.

The construction process can be illustrated best in the form of a flow chart to show the varied range of tasks and the order in which they are carried out. Figure 80 shows a typical flow chart of the construction process for a detached house (the contract documents of which are those studied in Topic 9).

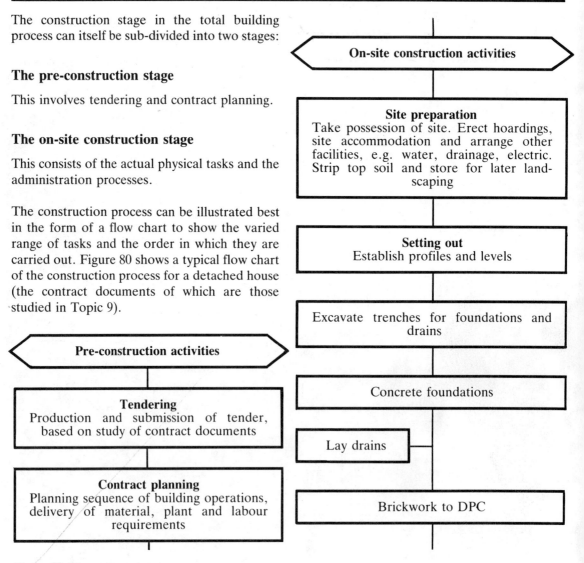

Figure 80 *The construction process*

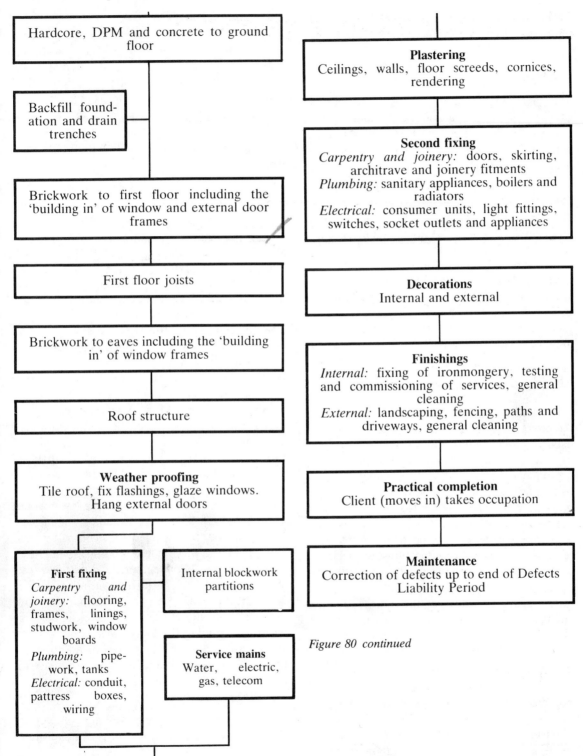

Hardcore, DPM and concrete to ground floor

Backfill foundation and drain trenches

Brickwork to first floor including the 'building in' of window and external door frames

First floor joists

Brickwork to eaves including the 'building in' of window frames

Roof structure

Weather proofing
Tile roof, fix flashings, glaze windows. Hang external doors

First fixing
Carpentry and joinery: flooring, frames, linings, studwork, window boards
Plumbing: pipework, tanks
Electrical: conduit, pattress boxes, wiring

Internal blockwork partitions

Service mains
Water, electric, gas, telecom

Plastering
Ceilings, walls, floor screeds, cornices, rendering

Second fixing
Carpentry and joinery: doors, skirting, architrave and joinery fitments
Plumbing: sanitary appliances, boilers and radiators
Electrical: consumer units, light fittings, switches, socket outlets and appliances

Decorations
Internal and external

Finishings
Internal: fixing of ironmongery, testing and commissioning of services, general cleaning
External: landscaping, fencing, paths and driveways, general cleaning

Practical completion
Client (moves in) takes occupation

Maintenance
Correction of defects up to end of Defects Liability Period

Figure 80 continued

The first of the *pre-construction stages* is tendering.

Tendering

The main way a building contractor obtains work is via the preparation and submission of tenders. There are *three* methods of tendering in common use: *open tendering*; *selective tendering*; *negotiated contracts*.

Open tendering

Architects place advertisements in newspapers and construction journals inviting contractors to tender for a particular project. Interested contractors will apply for the contract documents, and prepare and submit a tender within a specific time period. At the close of this tender period the quantity surveyor will open all the tenders and make recommendations to the architect and client as to the most suitable contractor, bearing in mind the contractor's expertise and his tender price.

Selective tendering

Architects establish a list of contractors with the expertise to carry out a specific project and will ask them to submit tenders for it. This list may be made up by the architect, simply from his experience of various contractors' expertise. Alternatively, advertisements may be placed in the newspapers and construction journals inviting contractors to apply to be included in a list of tenderers. From these applications, the architect will produce a short list of the most suitable contractors and ask them to tender. Again the quantity surveyor will open the returned tenders and make his recommendation to the architect and client.

Negotiated contracts

Here the architect selects and approaches suitable contractors and asks them to undertake the project. If the contractor is willing to undertake the project he will negotiate with the quantity surveyor to reach an agreed price.

Speculative building

In addition to tendering for work, many building contractors carry out work of a speculative nature. These are often termed speculative or 'spec' builders. This is where the building contractors on their own or as a part of a consortium, design and build a project for later sale, mainly private housing, but also offices, shops and industrial units. The building contractor is speculating or taking a chance that s/he will find a buyer (client) for the building.

Contract planning

On obtaining a contract for a building project, a contractor will prepare a programme which shows the sequence of work activities. In some cases an architect may stipulate that a programme of work is submitted by the contractor at the time of tendering; this gives the architect a measure of the contractor's organizing ability.

A programme will show the interrelationship between the different tasks and also when and for what duration resources such as materials, equipment and workforce are required. Once under way, the progress of the actual work can be compared with the target times contained in a programme. If the target times are realistic, a programme can be a source of motivation for the site management who will make every effort to stick to the programme and retrieve lost ground when required. There are a number of factors (some outside the management's control) which could lead to a programme modification. These factors include: bad weather; labour shortages; strikes; late material deliveries; variations to the contract; lack of specialist information; bad planning and site management etc. Therefore when determining the length of a contract, the contractor will normally make an addition of about 10% to the target completion date to allow for such eventualities.

Note: Contracts that run over the completion date involve extra costs, loss of profit and often time-penalty payments.

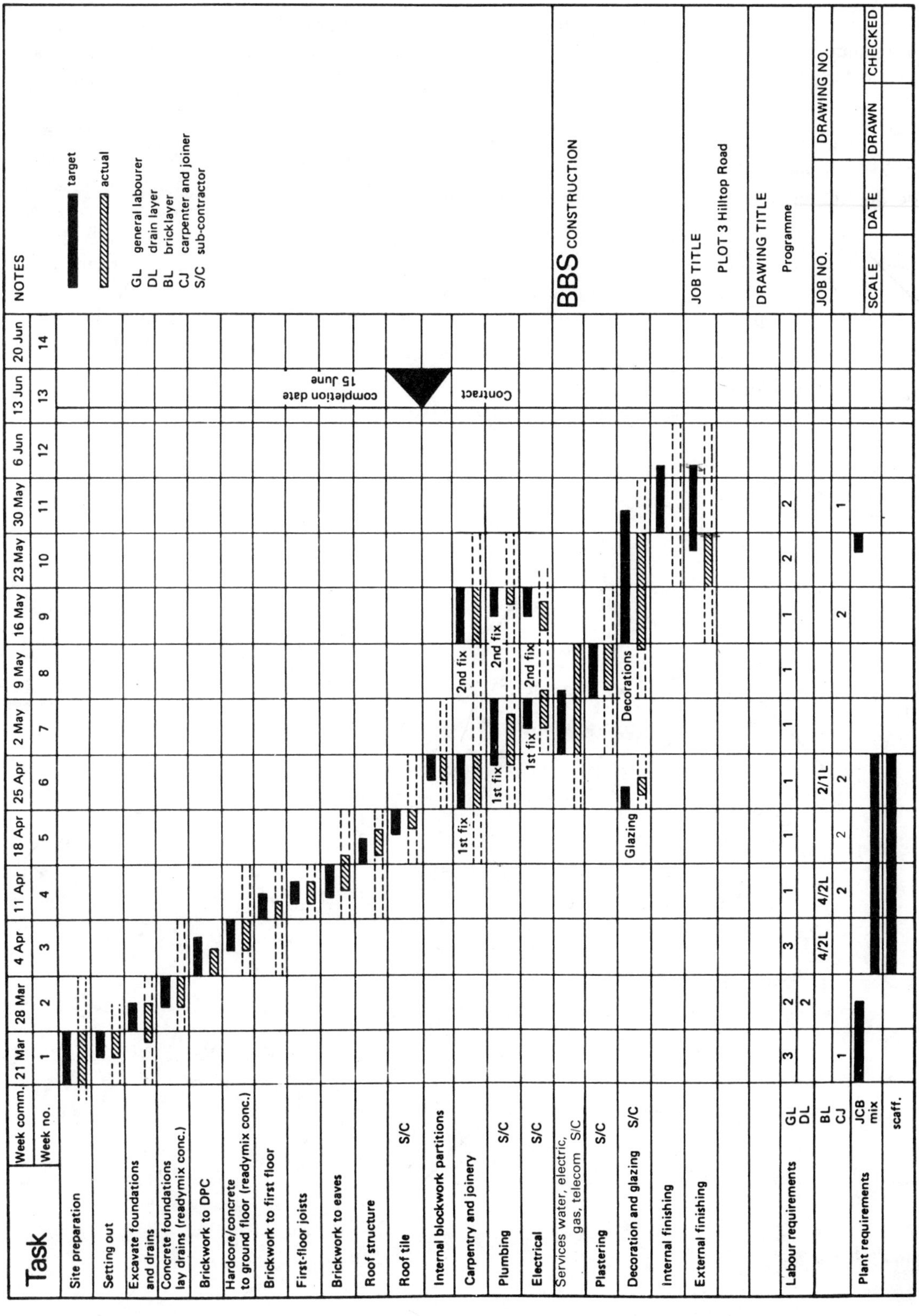

Task	Week comm.	21 Mar	28 Mar	4 Apr	11 Apr	18 Apr	25 Apr	2 May	9 May	16 May	23 May	30 May	6 Jun	13 Jun	20 Jun
	Week no.	1	2	3	4	5	6	7	8	9	10	11	12	13	14

Tasks (top to bottom):
- Site preparation
- Setting out
- Excavate foundations and drains
- Concrete foundations lay drains (readymix conc.)
- Brickwork to DPC
- Hardcore/concrete to ground floor (readymix conc.)
- Brickwork to first floor
- First-floor joists
- Brickwork to eaves
- Roof structure
- Roof tile S/C
- Internal blockwork partitions
- Carpentry and joinery
- Plumbing S/C
- Electrical S/C
- Services water, electric, gas, telecom S/C
- Plastering S/C
- Decoration and glazing S/C
- Internal finishing
- External finishing

Chart annotations: 1st fix, 2nd fix, Glazing, Decorations, Contract completion date 15 June

Labour requirements:
	1	2	3	4	5	6	7	8	9	10	11	12	13	14
GL / DL	3	2 / 2	3	1	1	1	1	1	1	2	2			
BL / CJ	1		4/2L	4/2L	2	2	2		2		1			

Plant requirements: JCB mix, scaff.

NOTES

■ target
▨ actual

GL general labourer
DL drain layer
BL bricklayer
CJ carpenter and joiner
S/C sub-contractor

BBS CONSTRUCTION

JOB TITLE PLOT 3 Hilltop Road

DRAWING TITLE Programme

JOB NO.		DRAWING NO.	
SCALE	DATE	DRAWN	CHECKED

Figure 81 *Bar/Gantt chart*

There are a number of different ways in which a programme can be produced and displayed. These include:

Bar charts
Line of balance charts
Critical path diagrams
Procedure diagrams

The most widely used and popular as far as the building contractor is concerned are the *bar* or *Gantt charts*. These charts are probably the most simple to use and understand. They are drawn up with the individual tasks listed in a vertical column on the left-hand side of the sheet and a horizontal time scale along the top. The target times of the individual tasks are shown by a horizontal bar. A second horizontal bar is shaded to show the work progress and the actual time taken for each task. Plant and labour requirements are often included along the bottom of the sheet. A typical bar/Gantt chart is shown in Figure 81. In addition to their use as an overall contract programme, bar charts can be used for short-term, weekly and monthly plans.

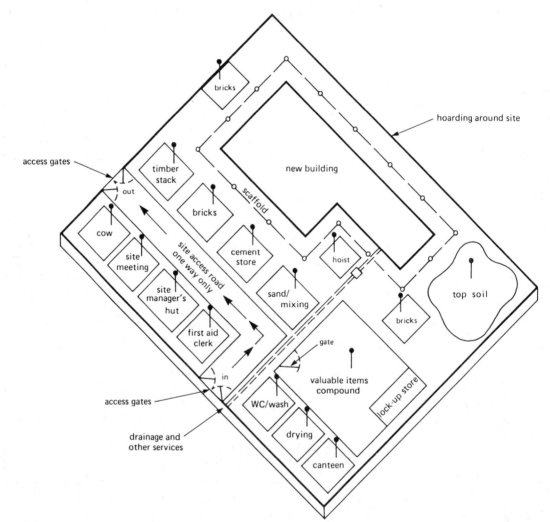

Figure 82   *Site layout*

On-site construction activities commence with the site layout.

Site layout

A building site can be seen as a temporary workshop and store from which the building contractor will erect the building. Site layouts can be planned on a pinboard using cardboard cut-outs held with map pins to represent the various requirements. The cut-outs can then be moved around until a satisfactory layout is achieved. See Figure 82 for a typical layout. A satisfactory layout is one which minimizes the movement of operatives, materials and plant during the course of construction while at the same time providing protection and security for materials.

Points to bear in mind when planning the layout are as follows:

1 Site accommodation must comply with the requirements of the Health and Safety at Work Act (HASAWA), Construction Regulations (health and welfare) and the National Working Rules for the building industry.
2 Materials storage areas should be convenient to the site access and the building itself. Different materials have different requirements. For example, timber in general should be stacked in 'stick' clear of the ground and covered with a tarpaulin; kiln-dried timber should be in a heated store; cement in a dry store; frames, pipes and drains etc. in a locked compound; and ironmongery, copper pipe, plumbing and electrical fittings in a locked secure store.
3 Consider phased deliveries of materials. It is often impossible to store on-site the complete stock required. Delay delivery of joinery fitments etc. Use can be made of the new building for storage.
4 On larger sites, provide work areas for formwork, reinforcement and pipework fabrication etc.; provide through routes for material deliveries, to avoid any reversing of lorries and traffic congestion; locate site management's accommodation away from the noise of the main building works; consider use of crane or hoist; consider use of security lighting and patrols.

Site administration

No building site could function effectively without a certain amount of day-to-day paper work and form filling. Those more likely to be encountered include:

Time sheets (Figure 83)
These are completed by each employee on a weekly basis, on which they give details of their hours worked and a description of the job or jobs carried out. Time sheets are used by the employer to determine wages and expenditure, gauge the accuracy of target programmes, provide information for future estimates and form the basis for claiming daywork payments. These sheets are sometimes completed by the foreman and timekeeper, especially on larger sites where a time clock is used.

Daywork sheets (Figure 84)
A common misconception is that daywork sheets are the same as time sheets; *they are not*. Daywork is work which is carried out without an estimate. This may range from emergency or repair work carried out by a jobbing builder to work that was unforeseen at the start of a major contract, for example, repairs, replacements, demolition, extra ground work, late alterations etc. Daywork sheets should be completed by the contractor, authorized by the clerk of works or architect and finally passed on to the quantity surveyor for inclusion in the next interim payment. This payment is made from the provisional contingency sum included in the Bill of Quantities for any unforeseen work. Details of the daywork procedures should be included in the contract conditions. A written architect's instruction is normally required before any work commences.

BBS CONSTRUCTION
WEEKLY TIME SHEET

Registered office

Name _____

Craft _____

Week commencing _____

	Job title	Description of work	Time: start/finish	total
MON				
TUE				
WED				
THUR				
FRI				
SAT				
SUN				

Details of expenses
(attach receipts)

Authorized by _____ Position _____

For office use only

Standard hours _____ at _____ = _____

Overtime hours _____ at _____ = _____

Overtime hours _____ at _____ = _____

Overtime hours _____ at _____ = _____

TOTAL = _____

Figure 83 *Time sheet*

BBS CONSTRUCTION
DAYWORK SHEET

Registered office

Sheet no. _____

Job title _____

Week commencing _____

Description of work

Labour	Name	Craft	Hours	Gross rate	Total
			Total labour		

Materials		Quantity	Rate	% Addition	
		Total materials			

Plant		Hours	Rate	% Addition	
		Total plant			

Note Gross labour rates include a percentage for overheads and profit as set out in the contract conditions.	Sub total	
	VAT (where applicable) _____ %	
	Total claim	

Site manager/foreman _____

Architect _____

Figure 84 *Daywork sheet*

BBS CONSTRUCTION
CONFIRMATION NOTICE

No._____ Date _____

Job title _____

From _____

To _____

Registered office

I confirm that today I have been issued with * verbal/written instructions from _____

Position _____

to carry out the following * daywork/variation to the contract

Additions

Omissions

Please issue your official * confirmation/variation order

Copies to head office

_____

_____

Signed _____

Position _____

* Delete as appropriate

Figure 85 *Confirmation notice*

BBS CONSTRUCTION
DAILY REPORT/SITE DIARY

Registered office

No._____ Date _____

Job title _____

Labour force on site		Labour force required	
Our employ	Subcontract	Our employ	Subcontract

Materials		Information	
Received (state delivery no.)	Required by (state requisition no.)	Received	Required by

Plant		Drawings	
Received (state delivery no.)	Required by (state requisition no.)	Received	Required by

Telephone calls To From	Site visitors
Accidents	Stoppages
Weather conditions	Temperature a.m. p.m.

Brief report of progress and other items of importance

Site manager/foreman _____

Note Send top copy daily to head office and retain carbon copy as an on-site record.

Figure 86 *Daily report/site diary*

BBS CONSTRUCTION
ORDER/REQUISITION

Registered office

No. _____

Date _____

To _____   From_____

Address   Site address

_____   _____

_____   _____

Please supply or order for delivery to the above site the following:

Description	Quantity	Rate		Date required by

Site manager/foreman _____

Note Please advise site within 24 hours of request if order cannot be fulfilled by the date required

Figure 87   *Order/requisition*

BBS CONSTRUCTION
DELIVERIES RECORD

Registered office

Week no. _____ Date _____

Job title _____

Delivery note no.	Date	Supplier	Description of delivery	For office use only	
				Rate	Value
			Total		

Site manager/foreman _____

Note Send weekly to head office with delivery notes

Figure 88 *Deliveries record*

Confirmation notice (Figure 85)

Where architects issue verbal instructions for daywork or variations, written confirmation of these instructions should be sought by the contractor, from the architect before any work is carried out. This precludes any misunderstanding and prevents disputes over payment at a later date.

Note: Although clerk of works' instructions are of an advisory or informative nature and do not normally involve extra payment, written confirmation of these should be received from the architect.

Daily report/site diary (Figure 86)

This is used to convey information back to head office and also to provide a source for future reference, especially should a problem or dispute arise later in the contract regarding verbal instructions, telephone promises, site visitors, delays or stoppages owing to late deliveries, late starts of sub-contractors or bad weather conditions. Like all reports, its purpose is to disclose or record facts; it should therefore be brief and to the point. Many contractors use a duplicate book for the combined daily report and site diary. After filling in, the top copy is sent to head office, the carbon copy being retained on-site. Some firms use two separate documents to fulfil the same function.

Orders/requisitions (Figure 87)

The majority of building materials are obtained through the firm's buyer, who at the estimating stage would have sought quotes from the various suppliers or manufacturers in order to compare prices, qualities and discounts. It is the buyer's responsibility to order and arrange phased deliveries of the required materials to coincide with the contract programme. Each job would be issued with a duplicate order/requisition book for obtaining sundry items from the firm's central stores or, in the case of a smaller builder, direct from the supplier. Items of plant would be requisitioned from the plant manager or plant hirers using a similar order/requisition book.

BBS CONSTRUCTION   **MEMO**

From _____   To _____

Subject _____   Date _____

Message

Figure 89   *Memorandum*

BBS CONSTRUCTION
EMPLOYEES
RECORD CARD

Registered office

Surname _____   Forenames _____

Permanent address _____   Temporary address _____

_____   _____

_____   _____

National Insurance number _____   Date of birth _____

Title of job _____

Commencement date _____

Other relevant details _____

_____

_____

_____

Documents received

P45 yes/no _____

Holiday card   yes/no   if yes state number and value of stamps

_____

_____

Documents issued

Statement of terms of employment   yes/no

The Company handbook   yes/no

(i) general policy and procedures
(ii) safety policy
(iii) disciplinary rules

I certify that the above details are correct and that I have been issued with the documents indicated.

Employees signature _____   Date _____

Personnel/training manager _____   Date _____

Figure 90 *Record card*

Full name	Title of job	

QUALIFICATIONS

Title	School/college	Dates from to

COURSES ATTENDED

Title	Location	Dates from to

SITE TRANSFER

From	To	Date/signature

ABSENCES FROM WORK

From	To	Reason

CONDUCT WARNINGS

Type	Reason	Date/signature

EMPLOYMENT TERMINATED

Reason	Comments	Date/signature

Figure 90 continued

BBS CONSTRUCTION
CONTRACT OF EMPLOYMENT

Registered office

STATEMENT OF MAIN TERMS OF EMPLOYMENT

Name of employer _____

Name of employee _____

Title of job _____

Statement issue date _____

Employment commencement date _____

Your hours of work, rates of pay, overtime, pay-day, holiday entitlement and payment, pension scheme, disciplinary procedures, notice and termination of employment and disputes procedure are in accordance with the following documents:

1 The National Working Rules for the Building Industry, approved by the National Joint Council for the Building Industry.

2 The Company wages register.

3 The Company handbook
  (i) general policy and procedures
  (ii) safety policy
  (iii) disciplinary rules

Copies of the above documents are available for your inspection on request at all site offices. Any future changes in the terms of employment will be made to these documents within one month of the change.

Figure 91   *Terms of employment*

Delivery records (Figure 88)

This forms a complete record of all the materials received on-site and should be filled in and sent to head office along with the other delivery notes on a weekly basis. This record is used to check deliveries before paying suppliers' invoices and also when determining the interim valuation.

Memorandum (memo) (Figure 89)

This is a printed form on which internal communications can be carried out. It is normally a brief note about the requirements of a particular job or details of an incoming inquiry (representative/telephone call) while a person was unavailable.

BBS CONSTRUCTION
DISCIPLINARY NOTICE

Registered office

FINAL WARNING

To _____ Date _____

Site _____

It is being brought to your attention that since the verbal warning given to you on _____

_____ by _____

concerning _____

* No significant improvement has been made/this conduct has been repeated.

This is a final warning* failure to show improvement/repetition of this conduct will result in your employment being terminated.

Personnel/training manager _____

* Delete as appropriate

Figure 92   *Final warning*

Employment conditions

The employment of any person is controlled by various Acts of Parliament. The main ones are:

Employment Protection (Consolidation) Act 1978.
Sex Discrimination Act 1975 (this embodies the Equal Pay Act 1970).
Race Relations Act 1976.

On engagement an employee record card, as shown in Figure 90, should be completed and signed by the employee. This card should be kept up to date during the employment to form a permanent record. The employee should be given a copy of the company's safety policy and a statement of the company's terms of employment. In addition, many company's issue their employees with a handbook containing details of the general policy and procedures, safety policy and general disciplinary rules.

Terms of employment

These terms of employment, a typical copy of which is shown in Figure 91, include details of commencement date; job title; hours of work; rates of pay; overtime; pay-day; holiday entitlement and pay; sick pay; pension scheme; disciplinary procedures; termination of employment; disputes procedure.

Disciplinary rules

This is a written statement outlining a company's disciplinary rules and dismissal procedures. It should be issued to all employees to ensure they are fully aware of the rules and procedures involved. They normally provide for verbal warnings of unsatisfactory conduct — for example, poor attendance, timekeeping or production and the failure to comply with working instructions or safety rules; this is followed by the final written warning. Where this written warning is not heeded, dismissal may follow. Figure 92 shows a typical final written warning.

Note: Verbal and written warnings are not required in cases of gross misconduct where instant dismissal can result. These cases are defined as: theft from the company; falsification of records for personal gain; and acts placing persons or property in danger.

National working rules

Most building operatives are employed using the wage rates, terms and conditions of employment as laid down in the National Working Rules for the building industry by the National Joint Council for the Building Industry (NJCBI). The main exceptions to this would be plumbing and mechanical services operatives whose terms of employment are negotiated by the Joint Industry Board (JIB), others who are employed under terms negotiated by the Building and Allied Trades Joint Industrial Council (BATJIC), and the self-employed.

National Joint Council for the building industry rules

The main functions of the council and their working rules are to:

1 fix basic wage rates;
2 determine conditions of employment;
3 settle disputes referred to them by both employers and operatives.

Basic rates and main conditions of employment are determined on a national level by the National Joint Council, which consists of representatives on the employers' side from the Building Employers Confederation (BEC) and other associated employers' organizations, and on the operatives' side from the trade unions. There are also local and regional committees that negotiate regional variations and additions to the National Working Rules. These rules are published in booklet form; they should be available for reference at your place of work and your college or they may be purchased through booksellers.

The main contents of this booklet are the twenty-seven National Working Rules which are grouped under the following headings:

Wages
Hours, conditions and holidays
Allowances
Retirement and death benefit
Apprentices/trainees
Scaffolders
Safety
General

In addition to these rules, the booklet contains certain explanatory notes, additional regional rules and variations, and also details of the annual holidays with the pay scheme which is operated by the Building and Civil Engineering Holidays Scheme Management Company.

Advisory, Conciliation and Arbitration Service (ACAS)

In the event of a dispute or grievance at work, the problem should first be taken to the foreman or site manager with the accompaniment of a

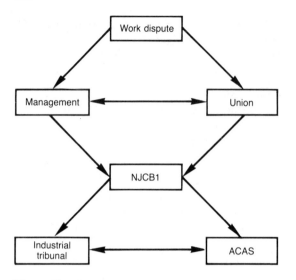

Figure 93   *Disputes procedure*

union representative if required. Where the problem cannot be solved at this level, it may be referred to a regional conciliation panel of the National Joint Council for settlement. If the outcome of this is unsatisfactory, individuals may refer their cases to the independent ACAS. Typical cases referred to ACAS include complaints in respect of: unfair dismissal; equal pay; sex or racial discrimination; suspension; redundancy; and trade union activities or membership (see Figure 93).

To make a complaint an individual must complete a form which is obtainable from Job Centres. The completed form should be sent to the Central Office of Industrial Tribunals who will pass a copy to ACAS. An ACAS conciliation officer will contact both sides in the dispute. If both parties are willing to accept conciliation, the officer will explain the views and legal position of each party to the other. In cases where partners cannot agree on a settlement, the matter will be decided by the industrial tribunal.

Note: Both parties, for example, employers and employees, can also get advice from ACAS without an official complaint having been made through the Central Office of Industrial Tribunals.

Self-assessment questions

Questions

1 Name and briefly explain the *two* major stages which together are termed 'the construction process'

2 Distinguish between 'open tendering' and 'selective tendering'

Your answer

_____

_____

_____

_____

_____

_____

_____

_____

_____

3 State the purpose of keeping a site diary and list *five* points that should be included in it

_____

_____

_____

_____

4 Explain the procedure that should be followed after an architect has issued verbal instructions to carry out additional works

_____

_____

_____

_____

5 Name the operations that should be carried out immediately prior to carpenters starting first fixing

_____

_____

_____

_____

6 Identify the organizations from the following abbreviations: (i) ACAS; (ii) BEC; (iii) NJCBI

_____

_____

_____

_____

7 Explain the difference between a daywork sheet and a time sheet

_____

_____

_____

_____

8 Briefly outline the procedure to be adopted in the event of a work dispute between a craftsman and his/her charge-hand

_____

_____

_____

_____

Building safety

Accidents

Definition

An accident is often described as a chance event or an unintentional act. This description is not acceptable as accidents don't 'just happen', they don't 'come out of the blue'; *they are caused*! A better *definition of an accident* is therefore:

An accident is an event causing injury or damage that could have been avoided by following correct methods and procedures.

Accident statistics

Each year there are some 40,000 accidents reported to the Health and Safety Executive and which occur during building-related activities in Great Britain (see Figure 94). Reported accidents are those which result in death, major injury, more than three day's absence from work, or are caused by a notifiable dangerous occurrence. That works out to about 800 accidents each week, 160 accidents each working day, 20 accidents each working hour or *one accident every three minutes*. That is, during the time it has taken you to read this far down the page, somewhere in Great Britain an accident has occurred, may be fatal, during a building activity, and which will be reported to the Health and Safety Executive (see p. 137). Of the 40,000 accidents reported to the Health and Safety Executive annually, about 140 prove to be fatal. That's almost three deaths each week.

Note: These figures are not intended to frighten you or put you off a future career in the building industry, but simply to make you aware of the hazards involved.

The Health and Safety Executive further break down these reported accident figures into the type of accident and the occupations of those involved.

Causes of accidents

Figure 95 illustrates the percentage distribution of fatal accidents overall; more than 50% of the accidents involved falls of persons. Figure 96 classifies the reported accidents by occupation.

Health and safety controls

In 1974 the Health and Safety at Work Act (HASAWA) was introduced. This Act became the main statutory legislation completely covering the health and safety of all persons at their place of work and protecting other people from risks occurring through work activities. All of the existing health and safety requirements operate in parallel with the HASAWA until they are gradually replaced by new regulations and codes of practices etc. made under the Act. The main health and safety legislation applicable to building sites and workshops is indicated in Table 6.

The *four* main objectives of the HASAWA are as follows:

1 To secure the health, safety and welfare of all persons at work.

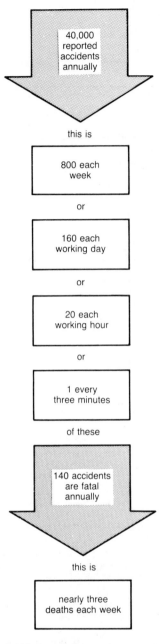

Figure 94   *Accident statistics*

2 To protect the general public from risks to health and safety arising out of work activities.
3 To control the use, handling, storage and transportation of explosives and highly flammable substances.

4 To control the release of noxious or offensive substances into the atmosphere.

These objectives can be achieved only by involving everyone in health and safety matters. This includes:

Employers and management
Employees
Self-employed
Designers, manufacturers and suppliers of equipment and materials.

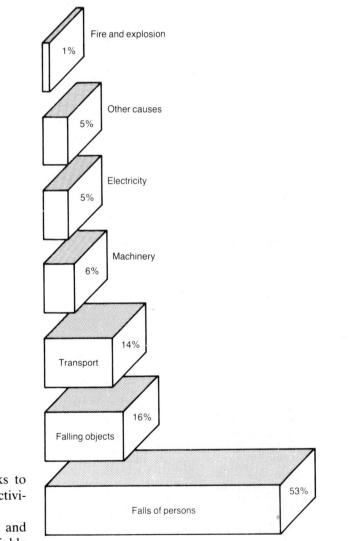

Figure 95   *Distribution of fatal accidents by cause*

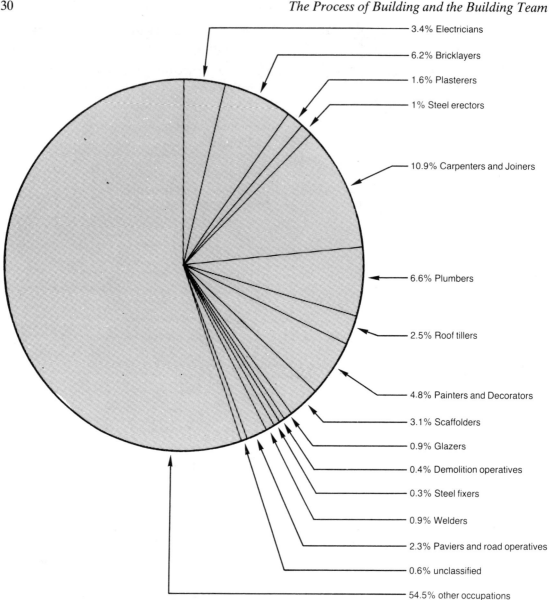

Figure 96   *Reported accidents by occupation*

Employers' and management's duties

Employers have a general duty to ensure the health and safety of their employees, visitors and the general public. This means that the employer must:

1 Provide and maintain a safe working working environment.
2 Ensure safe access to and from the workplace.

3 Provide and maintain safe machinery, equipment and methods of work.
4 Ensure the safe handling, transport and storage of all machinery, equipment and materials.
5 Provide their employees with the necessary information, instruction, training and supervision to ensure safe working.

Table 6 **Health and safety legislation**

Acts of Parliament	Regulations
Control of Pollution Act 1974	
Explosives Act 1875 and 1923	
Factories Act 1961	Abrasive Wheels Regulations 1970
	Asbestos Regulations 1969
	Construction (General Provisions) Regulations 1961
	Construction (Lifting Operations) Regulations 1961
	Construction (Health and Welfare) Regulations 1966
	Construction (Working Places) Regulations 1966
	Diving Operations Special Regulations 1960
	Electricity (Factories Act) Special Regulations 1908 and 1944
	Highly Flammable Liquids and Liquified Petroleum Gases Regulations 1972
	Lead Paint Regulations 1927
	Protection of Eyes Regulations 1974
	Woodworking Machines Regulations 1974
	Work in Compressed Air Special Regulations 1958 and 1960
Fire Precautions Act 1971	Fire Certificates (Special Premises) Regulations 1976
Food and Drugs Act 1955	Food Hygiene (General) Regulations 1970
Health and Safety at Work etc. Act 1974	Hazardous Substances (Labelling of Road Tankers) Regulations 1978
	Health and Safety (First Aid) Regulations 1981
	Notification of Accidents and Dangerous Occurrences Regulation 1980
	Control of Lead at Work Regulations 1980
	Safety Signs Regulations 1980
Mines and Quarries Act 1954	
Offices, Shops and Railway Premises Act 1963	

6 Prepare, issue to employees and update as required a written statement of the firm's safety policy.
7 Involve trade union safety representatives (where appointed) with all matters concerning the development, promotion and maintenance of health and safety requirements.

Note: An employer is not allowed to charge an employee for anything done, or equipment provided, to comply with any health and safety requirement.

Employees' duties
An *employee* is an individual who offers his or her skill and experience etc. to his or her employer in return for a monetary payment. It is

the duty of every employee while at work to comply with the following:

1 Take care at all times and ensure that his or her actions do not put at 'risk' himself or herself, workmates or any other person.
2 Co-operate with his or her employers to enable them to fulfil the employers' health and safety duties.
3 Use the equipment and safeguards provided by employers.
4 Never misuse or interfere with anything provided for health and safety.

Self-employed duties
The self-employed person can be thought of as both his or her employer and employee; therefore the duties under the Act are a

combination of those of the employer and employee.

Designers', manufacturers' and suppliers' duties

Under the Act, designers, manufacturers and suppliers as well as importers and hirers of equipment, machinery and materials for use at work have a duty to:

1 ensure that the equipment machinery or material is designed, manufactured and tested so that when it is used correctly no hazard to health and safety is created;
2 provide information or operating instructions as to the correct use, without risk, of their equipment, machinery or material

   [*Note:* Employers should ensure this information is passed on to their employees];

3 carry out research so that any risk to health and safety is eliminated or minimized as far as possible.

Enforcement

Under the HASAWA a system of control was established, aimed at reducing death, injury and ill-health. This system of control is represented by Figure 97. It consists of the Health and Safety Executive (HSE). The Executive is divided into

a number of specialist inspectorates or sections which operate from local offices situated throughout the country. From the local office, inspectors visit the individual workplaces.

Note: The section with the main responsibility for the building and construction industry is the Factory Inspectorate.

The Health and Safety Executive inspectors have been given wide powers of entry, examination and investigation in order to assist them in the enforcement of the HASAWA and earlier safety legislation. In addition to giving employers advice and information on health and safety matters, an inspector can do the following:

1 *Enter premises* In order to carry out investigations including the taking of measurements, photographs, recordings and samples. The inspector may require the premises to be left undisturbed while the investigations are taking place.

2 *Taking statements* An inspector can ask anyone questions relevant to the investigation and also require them to sign a declaration as to the truth of the answers.

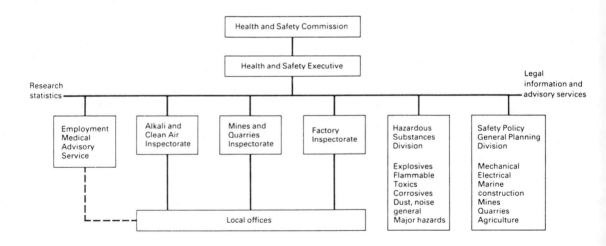

Figure 97 *Health and safety control*

HEALTH AND SAFETY EXECUTIVE
Health and Safety at Work etc. Act 1974, Sections 21, 23, and 24

IMPROVEMENT NOTICE

Serial No. **I**

Name and address (See Section 46)
To ....

(a) Delete as necessary
(a) Trading as ....

(b) Inspector's full name
I *(b)* ....
one of *(c)* ....

(c) Inspector's official designation
of *(d)* ....

(d) Official address
....   Tel no. ....

(e) ....
hereby give you notice that I am of the opinion that at

(e) Location of premises or place and activity
....

you, as *(a)* an employer/a self employed person wholly or partly in control of the premises,

(f) Other specified capacity
(f) ....
(a) .... are contravening/have contravened in circumstances that make it likely that the contravention will continue or be repeated

(g) Provisions contravened
(g) ....

The reasons for my said opinion are ....

....

and I hereby require you to remedy the said contraventions or, as the case may be, the matters occasioning them by ....

(h) ....
(a) in the manner stated in the attached schedule which forms part of the notice.

Signature .... Date ....

(h) Date
Being an inspector appointed by an instrument in writing made pursuant to Section 19 of the said Act and entitled to issue this notice.

(a) An improvement notice is also being served on ....

LP 1
of ....
related to the matters contained in this notice.

Dd 347139 5000 Pads 2/75 COH

NOTES

1   Failure to comply with an Improvement Notice is an offence as provided by Section 33 of this Act and renders the offender liable to a fine not exceeding £400 on summary conviction or to an unlimited fine on conviction on indictment and a further fine of not exceeding £50 per day if the offence is continued

2   An inspector has power to withdraw a notice or to extend the period specified in the notice before the end of the period specified in it. You should apply to the inspector who has issued the notice if you wish him to consider this, but you must do so before the end of the period given in it. *(Such an application is not an appeal against this notice.)*

3   The issue of this notice does not relieve you of any legal liability resting upon you for failure to comply with any provision of this or any other enactment, before or after the issue of this notice.

4   Your attention is drawn to the provision for appeal against this notice to an Industrial Tribunal. Details of the method of making an appeal are given below *(see also Section 24 of the Health and Safety at Work etc. Act 1974).*

(a)   Appeal can be entered against this notice to an Industrial Tribunal. The appeal should be sent to

(for England and Wales)   The Secretary of the Tribunals
Central Office of the Industrial Tribunals
93 Ebury Bridge Road LONDON SW1W 8RE

(for Scotland)   The Secretary of the Tribunals
Central Office of the Industrial Tribunals
Saint Andrew House
141 West Nile Street GLASGOW G1 2RU

(b)   The appeal must be commenced by sending in writing to the Secretary of the Tribunals a notice containing the following particulars :-

(1) The name of the appellant and his address for the service of documents.

(2) The date of the notice or notices appealed against; and the address of the premises or place concerned.

(3) The name and address *(as shown on the notice)* of the respondent.

(4) Particulars of the requirements or directions appealed against.

(5) The grounds of the appeal.

and

A form which may be used for appeal is attached

(c)   **Time limit for appeal**

A notice of appeal must be sent to the Secretary of the Tribunals within 21 days from the date of service on the appellant of the notice or notices appealed against, or within such further period as the tribunal considers reasonable in a case where it is satisfied that it was not reasonably practicable for the notice of appeal to be presented within the period of 21 days. If posted, the appeal should be sent by recorded delivery.

(d)   The entering of an appeal suspends the Improvement Notice until the appeal has been determined, but does not automatically alter the date given in this notice by which the matters contained in it must be remedied.

(e)   The rules for the hearing of an appeal are given in

The Industrial Tribunals (Improvement and Prohibition Notices Appeals) (S1 1974 No. 1925) for England and Wales.

The Industrial Tribunals (Improvement and Prohibition Notices Appeals) (S1 1974 No. 1926) for Scotland.

and

Figure 98   *Improvement notice*

HEALTH AND SAFETY EXECUTIVE
Health and Safety at Work etc. Act 1974, Sections 22–24

PROHIBITION NOTICE

Serial No **P**

Name and address (See Section 46)
To ....

(a) Delete as necessary
(a) Trading as ....

(b) Inspector's full name
I *(b)* ....

one of *(c)* ....

(c) Inspector's official designation
of *(d)* .... tel no ....

(d) Official address
hereby give you notice that I am of the opinion that the following activities,

namely – ....
....

which are *(a)* being carried on by you/about to be carried on by you/under your control

(e) Location of activity
at *(e)* ....

involve, or will involve *(a)* a risk/an imminent risk of serious personal injury.
I am further of the opinion that the said matters involve contravention of the following statutory provisions –
....

because ....
....

and I hereby direct that the said activities/shall not be carried on by you or under your control: *(a)* immediately/after

(f) ....

unless the said contraventions and matters included in the schedule, which forms part of this notice, have been remedied.

Signature .... Date ....

(f) Date
being an inspector appointed by an instrument in writing made pursuant to Section 19 of the said Act and entitled to issue this notice.

LP 2
Dd 347139 5000 Pads 2/75 COH

NOTES

1 Failure to comply with a Prohibition Notice is an offence as provided by Section 33 of this Act and renders the offender liable to a fine not exceeding £400 on summary conviction or to an unlimited fine or to imprisonment for a term not exceeding two years or both on conviction on indictment and a further fine of not exceeding £50 per day if the offence is continued.

2 An Inspector has power to withdraw a notice or to extend the period specified in the notice, before the end of the period specified in it. You should apply to the inspector who has issued the notice, if you wish him to consider this, but you must do so before the end of the period given in it. *(Such an application is not an appeal against this notice.)*

3 The issue of this Notice does not relieve you of any legal liability resting upon you for failure to comply with any provision of this or any other enactment, before or after the issue of this notice.

4 Your attention is drawn to the provision for appeal against the notice to an Industrial Tribunal. Details of the method of making an appeal are given below *(see also Section 24 of the Health and Safety at Work etc. Act 1974).*

   (a) Appeal can be entered against this notice to an Industrial Tribunal. The appeal should be sent to

   (for England and Wales)   The Secretary of the Tribunals
                              Central Office of the Industrial Tribunals
                              93 Ebury Bridge Road LONDON SW1W 8RE

   (for Scotland)   The Secretary of the Tribunals
                              Central Office of the Industrial Tribunals
                              Saint Andrew House
                              141 West Nile Street GLASGOW G1 2RU

   (b) The appeal must be commenced by sending in writing to the Secretary of the Tribunals a notice containing the following particulars –
   (1) The name of the appellant and his address for the service of documents.
   (2) The date of the notice or notices appealed against and the address of the premises or place concerned.
   (3) The name and address (as shown on the notice) of the respondent.
   (4) Particulars of the requirements or directions appealed against.
   (5) The grounds of the appeal.
   A form which may be used for appeal is attached.

   (c) Time limit for appeal

   A notice of appeal must be sent to the Secretary of the Tribunals within 21 days from the date of service on the appellant of the notice or notices appealed against, or within such further period as the tribunal considers reasonable in a case where it is satisfied that it was not reasonably practicable for the notice of appeal to be presented within the period of 21 days. If posted the appeal should be sent by recorded delivery.

   (a) The entering of an appeal does not have the effect of suspending this notice. Application can be made for the suspension of the notice to the Secretary of the Tribunals, but the notice continues in force until a Tribunal otherwise directs. An application for suspension of the notice must be in writing and must set out –

   (a) The case number of the appeal, (if known, or particulars sufficient to identify it and

   (b) The grounds on which the application is made, it may accompany the appeal.

   (e) The rules for the hearing of an appeal are given in –

   The Industrial Tribunals (Improvement and Prohibition Notices Appeals) Regulations 1974 (SI 1974 No. 1925) for England and Wales.

   and

   The Industrial Tribunals (Improvement and Prohibition Notices Appeals) (Scotland) Regulations 1974 (SI 1974 No. 1926) for Scotland.

SPECIMEN

Figure 99 *Prohibition notice*

3 *Check records* All books, records and documents required by legislation must be made available for inspection and copying.

4 *Give information* An inspector has a duty to give employees or their safety representative information about the safety of their workplace and details of any action he proposes to take. This information must also be given to the employer.

5 *Demand* The inspector can demand the seizure, dismantling, neutralizing or destruction of any machinery, equipment, material or substance that is likely to cause immediate serious personal injury.

6 *Issue an improvement notice (Figure 98)* This requires the responsible person (employer or manufacturer etc.) to put right within a specified period of time any minor hazard or infringement of legislation.

7 *Issue a prohibition notice (Figure 99)* This requires the responsible person to immediately stop any activities which are likely to result in serious personal injury. This ban on activities continues until the situation is corrected. An appeal against an improvement or prohibition notice may be made to an industrial tribunal.

8 *Prosecute* All persons, including employers, employees, the self-employed, designers, manufacturers and suppliers who fail to comply with their safety duty may be prosecuted in a magistrates' court or in certain circumstances in the higher court system. Conviction can lead to unlimited fines, or a prison sentence, or both.

The construction regulations

These are the regulations made under the Factories Act 1961 which are specific to construction operations. They are divided into four parts, each dealing with a different aspect of work.

Construction (General Provisions) Regulations 1961 Set out minimum standards to promote a good level of general safety.

Construction (Lifting Operations) Regulations 1961 Lay down requirements regarding the manufacture, maintenance and inspection of lifting appliances used on site (gin wheels, cranes and hoists etc.)

Construction (Health and Welfare) Regulations 1966 Set out minimum provisions for site accommodation, washing facilities, sanitary conveniences and protective clothing.

Constructions (Working Places) Regulations 1966 Control the erection, use and inspection of scaffolds and other similar temporary structures.

Safety documentation

In order to comply with the various safety legislation, an employer is required to:

Display notices and certificates
Notify relevant authorities
Keep relevant records

Notices and certificates

An employer must prominently display on-site, in the workshop, or in an office where the employees attend, a number of notices and certificates, the main ones being (where applicable):

1 Copy of the certificate of insurance; this is required under the Employers' Liability (Compulsory Insurance) Act 1969.
2 Copy of fire certificate.
3 Abstract of the Factories Act 1961 for building operations and works of engineering constructions.
4 Details of the area Health and Safety Executive Inspectorate; the employment medical adviser and the site safety supervisor should be indicated on this form.
5 Abstract of the Offices, Shops and Railway Premises Act 1963.

Health
and
Safety
Executive

F 10
Reprinted December 1979

For official use

Registered...............................

Visited.......................................

FACTORIES ACT 1961

Notice of building operations or works of engineering construction*

1   Name of person, firm, or company
    undertaking the operations or works.

2   State whether main contractor or
    sub-contractor.

3   Trade of the person, firm or company
    undertaking the operations or works.

4   Address of registered office (in case
    of company) or of principal place of
    business (in other cases).

5   Address to which communications
    should be sent (if different from above).

6   Place where the operations or works
    are carried on.

7   Name of Local Government District
    Council (in Scotland, County Council
    or Burgh Town Council) within whose
    district the operations or works are
    situated.

8   Telephone No. (if any) of the site.

9   How many workers are you likely
    to employ on the site?

10 Approximate date of commencement.

11 Probable duration of work.

12 Is mechanical power being, or to be,
    used? If so, what is its nature (e.g.
    electric, steam, gas or oil)?

13 Nature of operations or works
    carried on:

(a) Building operations *(tick items which apply)*

     Construction ....

     Maintenance .... } of

     Demolition ....

     Industrial building ....

     Commercial or public building ....

     Dwellings over 3 storeys ....

     Dwellings of 3 storeys or less ....

     Others ....

(b) Works of engineering construction *(specify type)*

     I hereby give notice that I am undertaking the building operations or works of engineering construction specified above.

Signature   Date

NOTE

* Any person undertaking any building operations or works of engineering construction to which the Act applies is required by the Act, not later than seven days after the beginning of any such operations or works, to serve on the Inspector for the district a written notice giving particulars specified in section 127(6) unless (a) they are operations or works which the person undertaking them has reasonable grounds for believing will be completed in less than six weeks, or (b) notice has already been given to the Inspector in respect of building operations or works of engineering construction already in progress at the same place. This form should be filled up and sent to HM Inspector of Factories for the district in which the operations or works are carried on.

572 8033375 200M 12/79 HGW 752

Figure 100   *Notice of building operations*

Health and Safety Executive
Health and Safety at Work etc Act 1974
Reporting of Injuries,Diseases and Dangerous Occurrences Regulations 1985

Report of an injury or dangerous occurrence

- Full notes to help you complete this form are attached.
- This form is to be used to make a report to the enforcing authority under the requirements of Regulations 3 or 6.
- Completing and signing this form does not constitute an admission of liability of any kind, either by the person making the report or any other person.
- If more than one person was injured as a result of an accident, please complete a separate form for each person.

A **Subject of report** *(tick appropriate box or boxes)* — *see note 2*

Fatality	Specified major injury or condition	"Over three day" injury	Dangerous occurrence	Flammable gas incident (fatality or major injury or condition)	Dangerous gas fitting
1	2	3	4	5	6

B **Person or organisation making report** (ie person obliged to report under the Regulations) — *see note 3*

Name and address —

Post code —

Name and telephone no. of person to contact —

Nature of trade, business or undertaking —

If in construction industry, state the total number of your employees —

and indicate the role of your company on site *(tick box)* —

Main site contractor	Sub contractor	Other
7	8	9

If in farming, are you reporting an injury to a member of your family? *(tick box)*
Yes   No

C **Date, time and place of accident, dangerous occurrence or flammable gas incident** — *see note 4*

Date [   ] [   ] 19 [   ]   Time —
day month year

Give the name and address if different from above —

Where on the premises or site —
and
Normal activity carried on there

ENV

Complete the following sections D, E, F & H if you have ticked boxes, 1, 2, 3 or 5 in Section A. Otherwise go straight to Sections G and H.

D **The injured person** — *see note 5*

Full name and address —

Age [ ] Sex [ ] (M or F)	Status *(tick box)* —	Employee	Self employed	Trainee (YTS)
		10	11	12
		Trainee (other)		Any other person
		13		14

Trade, occupation or job title —

Nature of injury or condition and the part of the body affected —

F2508 (rev 1/86)   *continued overleaf*

Figure 101   *Report of accident*

E Kind of accident - *see note 6*

Indicate what kind of accident led to the injury or condition (*tick one box*) —

Contact with moving machinery or material being machined ☐ 1	Injured whilst handling lifting or carrying ☐ 5	Trapped by something collapsing or overturning ☐ 8	Exposure to an explosion ☐ 12
Struck by moving, including flying or falling, object. ☐ 2	Slip, trip or fall on same level ☐ 6	Drowning or asphyxiation ☐ 9	Contact with electricity or an electrical discharge ☐ 13
Struck by moving vehicle ☐ 3	Fall from a height* ☐ 7	Exposure to or contact with a harmful substance ☐ 10	Injured by an animal ☐ 14
Struck against something fixed or stationary ☐ 4	*Distance through which person fell ☐ (metres)	Exposure to fire ☐ 11	Other kind of accident (give details in Section H) ☐ 15

Spaces below are for office use only. ☐

F Agent(s) involved — *see note 7*

Indicate which, if any, of the categories of agent or factor below were involved (*tick one or more of the boxes*) —

Machinery/equipment for lifting and conveying ☐ 1	Process plant, pipework or bulk storage ☐ 5	Live animal ☐ 9	Ladder or scaffolding ☐ 13
Portable power or hand tools ☐ 2	Any material, substance or product being handled, used or stored. ☐ 6	Moveable container or package of any kind ☐ 10	Construction formwork, shuttering and falsework ☐ 14
Any vehicle or associated equipment/ machinery ☐ 3	Gas, vapour, dust, fume or oxygen deficient atmosphere ☐ 7	Floor, ground, stairs or any working surface ☐ 11	Electricity supply cable, wiring, apparatus or equipment ☐ 15
Other machinery ☐ 4	Pathogen or infected material ☐ 8	Building, engineering structure or excavation/underground working ☐ 12	Entertainment or sporting facilities or equipment ☐ 16
			Any other agent ☐ 17

Describe briefly the agents or factors you have indicated —

[ ]

G Dangerous occurrence or dangerous gas fitting — *see notes 8 and 9*

Reference number of dangerous occurrence [ ]   Reference number of dangerous gas fitting [ ]

H Account of accident, dangerous occurrence or flammable gas incident - *see note 10*

Describe what happened and how. In the case of an accident state what the injured person was doing at the time —

[ ]

☐
☐

Signature of person making report [ ]   Date [ ]

Figure 101 continued

6 The Woodworking Machines Regulations 1974.

7 The Abrasive Wheels Regulations 1970 and cautionary notice.

8 The Electricity (Factories Act) Special Regulations 1908 and 1944. Electric shock (first aid) placard.

9 The Asbestos Regulations 1969.

10 The Highly Flammable Liquids and Liquified Petroleum Gases Regulations 1972.

Notifications

The following are the main notifications required. They are usually submitted on standard forms obtainable from the relevant authority.

1 The commencement of building operations or works of engineering constructions that are likely to last more than six weeks (see Figure 100).

2 The employment of persons in an office or shop for more than 21 hours a week.

3 The employment or transfer of young persons (under 18 years of age) must be notified to the local careers office.

4 Accidents resulting in death or major injuries or notifiable dangerous occurrences, or more than three days absence from work (see Figure 101). Major injuries can be defined as most fractures, amputations, loss of sight or any other injury involving a stay in hospital.

PART 2

Appointment of persons to mount abrasive wheels (regulation 9)

	APPOINTMENT			REVOCATION	
Name of person appointed	Class or description of abrasive wheels for which appointment is made (*See Note* 7)	Date of appointment	Signature of occupier or his agent	Date of revocation of appointment (*See Note* 5)	Signature of occupier or his agent
(1)	(2)	(3)	(4)	(5)	(6)

3

Figure 102 *Abrasive wheel register*

Many incidents can be defined as notifiable dangerous occurrences but in general they include the collapse of a crane, hoist, scaffolding or building, an explosion or fire, or the escape of any substance that is liable to cause a health hazard or major injury to any person.

5 A poisoning or suffocation incident resulting in acute ill health requiring medical treatment.

6 Application for a fire certificate, if required under the Fire Certificates (Special Premises) Regulations 1976.

Records

Employers are required to keep various records. These should be kept ready for inspection on-site or at the place of work and should include the following:

1 The general register for building operations and works of engineering constructions. This is used to record details of the site or workshop and the nature of work taking place, any cases of poisoning or disease and the employment or transfer of young persons.

2 An accident book in which details of all accidents are recorded.

3 A record of accidents, dangerous occurrences and ill-health enquiries (Form F2509). Entries in the record must be made whenever the Health and Safety Executive is notified of an accident resulting in death, major injury or a notifiable dangerous occurrence and when

Name or title of employer or contractor ____________

Factories Act 1961

Construction (Working Places) Regulations 1966

SECTION A

Address of site ____________

Work commenced—Date ____________

SCAFFOLD INSPECTIONS

Reports of results of inspections under Regulations 22 of scaffolds, including boatswain's chairs, cages, skips and similar plant or equipment (and plant or equipment used for the purposes thereof)

Location and description of scaffold, etc. and other plant or equipment inspected (1)	Date of inspection (2)	Result of inspection State whether in good order (3)	Signature (or, in case where signature is not legally required, name) of person who made the inspection (4)

NOTES TO SECTION A

(1) *Short check list—at each inspection check that your scaffolding does not have these faults:*

		Week 1	Week 2	Week 3	Week 4
FOOTINGS	Soft and uneven No base plates No sole boards Undermined				
STANDARDS	Not plumb Joined at same height Wrong spacing Damaged				
LEDGERS	Not level Joint in same bays Loose Damaged				

		Week 1	Week 2	Week 3	Week 4
BRACING 'Facade and ledger'	Some missing Loose Wrong fittings				
PUTLOGS and TRANSOMS	Wrongly spaced Loose Wrongly supported				
COUPLINGS	Wrong fitting Loose Damaged No check couplers				
BRIDLES	Wrong spacing Wrong couplings Weak support				

		Week 1	Week 2	Week 3	Week 4
TIES	Some missing Loose				
BOARDING	Bad boards Trap boards Incomplete Insufficient supports				
GUARD RAILS & TOE BOARDS	Wrong height Loose Some missing				
LADDERS	Damaged Insufficient length Not tied				

(2) *This check list is not part of the report required by Regulation 22: see also para 5 of Notes and Regulation 22 on page (ii) of cover and Notes on page 13.*

Figure 103 *Scaffold form*

enquiries are made by the Department of Health and Social Security concerning claims by employees for industrial disease.

4 Register for the purposes of the Abrasive Wheels Regulations 1970. A register used to record details of persons appointed to mount abrasive wheels (see Figure 102).

5 Records of inspections, examinations and special tests. This is a booklet of forms on which details of inspections etc. on scaffolding, excavations, earthworks and lifting appliances must be recorded. (See Figure 103 for scaffold form).

6 Record of reports. This provides forms for recording the thorough examination of lifting appliances, hoists, chains, ropes and other lifting gear and also the heat treatment of chains and lifting gear.

7 Register and certificate of shared welfare arrangements. To be completed where an employer, normally the main contractor, provides the welfare facilities for another employer (sub-contractor).

8 Certificates of tests and examinations of various lifting appliances. These are records of the weekly, monthly or other periodic tests and examinations required by the construction regulations as follows:

Cranes
Hoists
Other lifting appliances
Wire ropes
Chains, slings and lifting gear

Safety signs

Formally there were many vastly different safety signs in use. British Standards BS 5378: Part One: 1980: Safety Signs and Colours introduced a standard system of giving health and safety information with a minimum use of words. Its purpose is to establish an internationally understood system of safety signs and safety colours which draws attention to objects and situations that do, or could, affect health and safety. Details of these signs and typical examples of use are given in Table 7.

General safety

It should be the aim of everyone to prevent accidents. Remember, you are required by law to be aware and fulfil your duties under the Health and Safety at Work Act.

The main contribution you as an operative can make towards the prevention of accidents is to work in the safest possible manner at all times, thus ensuring that your actions do not put at risk yourself, your workmates or the general public.

On-site and in the workshop

A safe working area is a tidy working area. All unnecessary obstructions which may create a hazard should be removed, e.g. off-cuts of material, unwanted materials, disused items of plant, and the extraction or flattening of nails from discarded pieces of timber. Therefore:

1 Clean up your workbench/work area periodically as off-cuts and shavings are potential tripping and fire hazards.

2 Careful disposal of materials from heights is essential. They should always be lowered safely and not thrown or dropped from scaffolds and window openings etc. Even a small bolt or fitting dropped from a height can penetrate a person's skull and almost certainly lead to brain damage or death.

3 Ensure your tools are in good condition. Blunt cutting tools, loose hammer heads, broken or missing handles and mushroom heads must be repaired immediately or the use of the tool discontinued (see Figure 104).

4 When moving materials and equipment always look at the job first; if it is too big for you then get help. Look out for splinters, nails, and sharp or jagged edges on the items

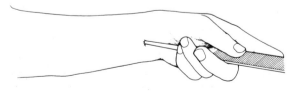

Figure 104 *Missing file handle (unsafe practice)*

Table 7 **Safety signs**

Purpose	Sign	Definition	Examples for use
Prohibition		A sign prohibiting certain behaviour	
Caution		A sign giving warning of certain hazards	
Safe condition		A sign providing information about safe conditions	
Mandatory		A sign indicating that a special course of action is required	
Supplementary		A sign with text. Can be used in conjunction with a safety sign to provide additional information.	

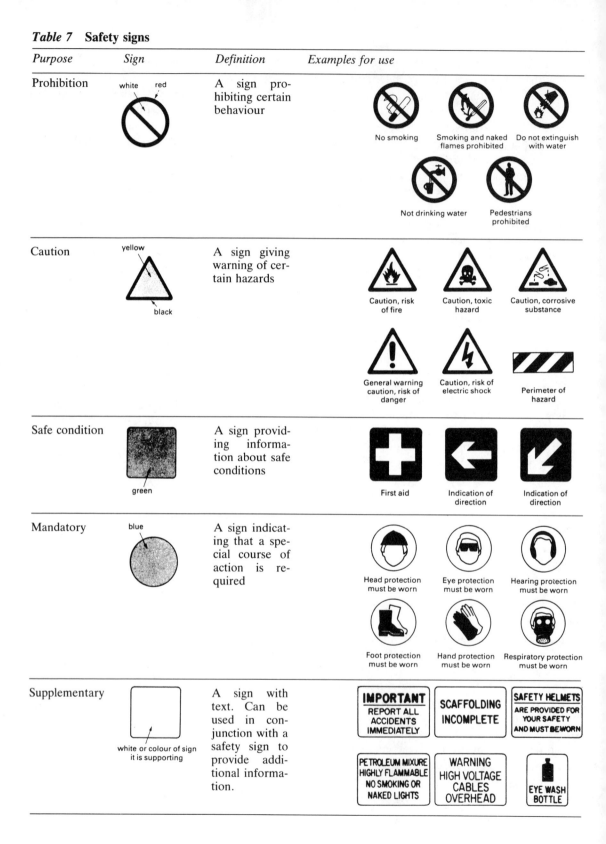

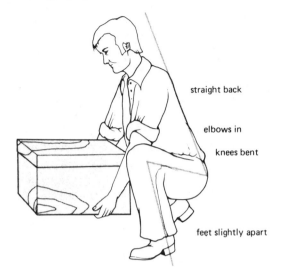

Figure 105   *Correct lifting position*

straight back

elbows in

knees bent

feet slightly apart

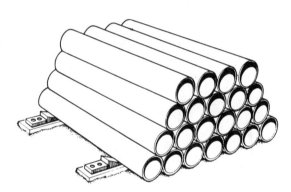

Figure 106   *Acceptable horizontal storage of cylinders, pipes, drums, etc.*

drums etc. should be wedged or chocked to prevent rolling. Never climb on a stack or remove material from its sides or bottom (see Figure 106).

6 Excavations and inspection chambers should be either protected by a barrier or covered over completely to prevent people carelessly falling into them (see Figure 107).

7 Extra care is needed when working at heights. Ladders should be of sufficient length for the work in hand and should be in good condition and not split, twisted or with rungs missing. They should also be used at a working angle of 75 degrees and securely tied at the top. This angle is a slope of four

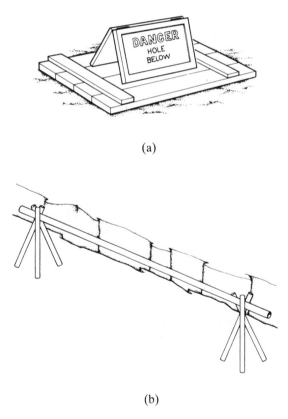

(a)

(b)

Figure 107   *(a) Small holes and excavations should be covered with timber or sheet metal. (b) Trenches should be fenced off with scaffold tubes*

to be moved. Always lift with your back straight, elbows tucked in, knees bent and feet slightly apart (see Figure 105). When putting an item down ensure that your hands and fingers will not be trapped.

5 Materials must be stacked on a firm foundation; stacks should be of reasonable height so as to allow easy removal of items. They should also be bonded to prevent collapse and battered to spread the load. Pipes and

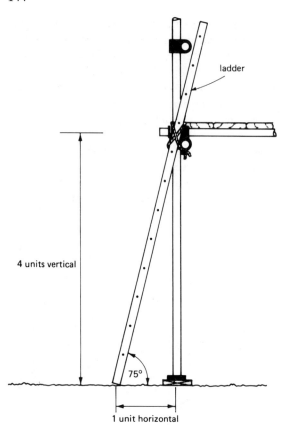

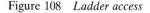

Figure 108   *Ladder access*

10 Working with electrical and compressed-air equipment brings additional hazards as they are both potential killers. Installations and equipment should be checked regularly by qualified personnel; if anything is incomplete, damaged, frayed, worn or loose, do not use, but return to stores for attention. Ensure cables and hoses are kept as short as possible and routed safely out of the way to prevent risk of tripping or damage.

11 Always wear the correct protective equipment for the work in hand. Safety helmets and safety footwear should be worn at all times. Wear ear protectors when carrying out noisy activities, and safety goggles when carrying out any operation that is likely to produce dust, chips or sparks, etc. Dust

Figure 109   *Securing a ladder with stakes and guy ropes*

vertical units to one horizontal unit. (See Figure 108). Where a fixing at the top is not possible, an alternative is the stake-and-guy rope method shown in Figure 109.

8 Scaffolds should be inspected before working on them. Check to see that all components are there and in good condition—not bent, twisted, rusty, split, loose or out of plumb and level. Also ensure that the base has not been undermined or is too close to excavations (see Figure 110). If in doubt do not use, and have it looked at by an experienced scaffolder.

9 When working on roofs, roofing ladders or crawl boards should be used to provide safe access and/or avoid falling through fragile coverings.

masks or respirators should be worn where dust is being produced or fumes are present, and gloves when handling materials. Wet-weather clothing is necessary for inclement conditions. Many of these items must be supplied free of charge by your employer.

12 Care should be taken with personal hygiene which is just as important as physical protection. Some building materials have an irritant effect on contact with the skin. Some are poisonous if swallowed, while others can result in narcosis if their vapour or powder is inhaled. These harmful effects can be avoided by taking proper precautions: follow the manufacturer's instructions; avoid inhaling fumes or powders; wear a barrier cream; thoroughly wash your hands before eating, smoking and after work.

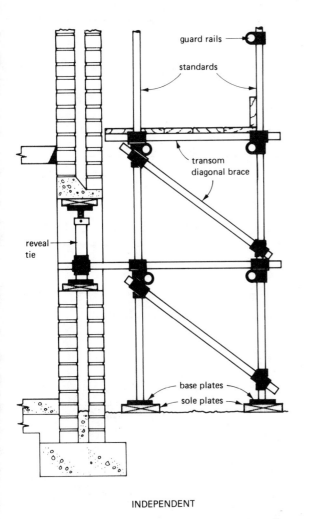

INDEPENDENT

PUTLOG

Figure 110   *Putlog and independent scaffolds*

Self-assessment questions

Questions   *Your answer*

1 State *two* of the main objectives of the Health and Safety
   at Work Act

   _____

   _____

   _____

   _____

2 Define what constitutes a
   reported accident and state to
   whom it is reported

   _____

   _____

   _____

   _____

3 List *two* duties of each of the
   following under the Health
   and Safety at Work Act:
   (i) Employers; (ii) employees

   _____

   _____

   _____

   _____

4 Name *two* notices or certificates that must be displayed
   on-site

   _____

   _____

   _____

   _____

5 List the main powers of a
   Health and Safety Executive
   inspector

   _____

   _____

   _____

   _____

6 What information must be
   recorded in a general register?

   _____

   _____

   _____

   _____

7 Describe the purpose of an improvement notice

_____

_____

_____

_____

8 Define the term 'accident'

_____

_____

_____

_____

9 A safety sign that is contained in a yellow triangle with a black border is:
   (a) prohibiting certain behaviour
   (b) warning of certain hazards
   (c) providing information about safe conditions
   (d) indicating that safety equipment must be worn?

   ⌐ a ⌐   ⌐ b ⌐   ⌐ c ⌐   ⌐ d ⌐

10 Over 50% of fatal accidents in the building industry involve:
   (a) machinery
   (b) electric shock
   (c) falls
   (d) transport?

   ⌐ a ⌐   ⌐ b ⌐   ⌐ c ⌐   ⌐ d ⌐

Topic 12

Assignment two

Approximately three hours are required to answer this assignment

Assignments are intended to illustrate some of the day-to-day problems/enquiries which you as a member of the building industry may encounter.

For the purposes of this assignment you should assume that you are employed as a site agent by a company that specializes in house building. Your next contract is a small estate of four-bedroomed detached houses and two-bedroomed detached bungalows.

You should attempt all six tasks of this assignment, which are based on the documents illustrated in Figures 111 to 114. Illustrate your answers with sketches where appropriate.

Task one

1 Prepare a flow chart to show (in the order that they are carried out) the main on-site construction tasks for plot No. 6, commencing with the setting out, and finishing at practical completion

Task two

2 Indicate on the site plan the suggested positioning of the following temporary accommodation: (i) site agent/foremans office; (ii) WC/washroom; (iii) canteen/drying room; (iv) stores

3 State the provisions to be made on the site for storing the following items: (i) cement; (ii) timber joists; (iii) paint; (iv) copper pipes; (v) plumbing and electric fittings

Task three

4 Name *three* notifications and *three* records that must be given or kept during construction operations, in order to comply with health and safety legislation

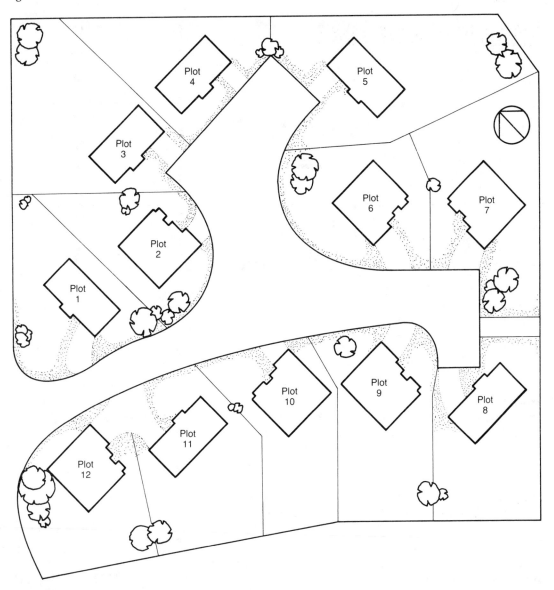

Figure 111   *Estate plan*

5 Identify *four* site operations where you would insist on the use of protective equipment. Name the item of equipment in each case _____

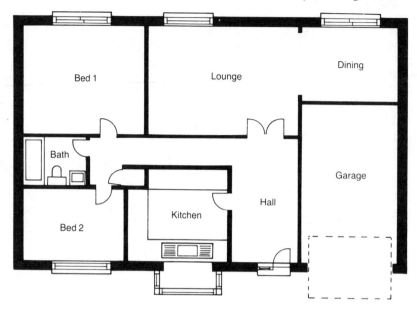

Figure 112   *The lakeside bungalow plan*

Figure 113   *The Whiteman house plans*

Title block (drawing):

BBS DESIGN

JOB TITLE — Lakeside Estate
DRAWING TITLE — Schedule for sanitary appliances
JOB NO. —
DRAWING NO. —
SCALE — | DATE — | DRAWN — | CHECKED —

Description	P2 Kitchen	P2 Cloaks	P2 Bath	P2 En-suite	P6 Kitchen	P6 Cloaks	P6 Bath	P6 En-suite	P7 Kitchen	P7 Cloaks	P7 Bath	P7 En-suite	P9 Kitchen	P9 Cloaks	P9 Bath	P9 En-suite	P10 Kitchen	P10 Cloaks	P10 Bath	P10 En-suite	P12 Kitchen	P12 Cloaks	P12 Bath	P12 En-suite	Notes
ITEM (see range)																									
Inset sink	X				X				X				X				X				X				
Waste disposal unit	X								X												X				
Close Couple WC		X	X	X		X	X	X		X	X	X		X	X	X		X	X	X		X	X	X	
Bidet				X				X				X				X				X				X	
Pedestal wash basin			X	X			X	X			X	X			X	X			X	X			X	X	
Wall hung corner basin		X				X				X				X				X				X			
Bath			X				X				X				X				X				X		
Shower tray				X				X				X				X				X				X	
STYLE (see range)																									
Anne		X	X	X		X	X	X						X	X	X									
Sarah										X	X	X						X	X	X		X	X	X	
James	X				X				X				X				X				X				
Single drainer					X								X				X								
Double drainer	X								X												X				
COLOUR																									
Penthouse Red						X	X	X																	
Indian ivory														X	X	X						X	X	X	
Honeysuckle		X	X	X																					
White	X				X				X	X	X	X	X				X	X	X	X	X				
BRASS WORK																									
Chrome plated		X	X	X						X	X	X						X	X	X					
Gold plated						X	X	X						X	X	X						X	X	X	

Figure 114 Sanitary appliance schedule

Task four

6 Using the schedule of sanitary
appliances take off and produce a list of the items required for plot No. 10

_____

_____

_____

_____

Task five

7 The finishing paint colour for
each plot's external doors is to
be determined by the compass
orientation of their front entrance door:

North facing — red
South facing — green
East   facing — brown
West   facing — blue

Using the compass orientation
shown in Figure 115, and the
main drawing, determine and
produce a list to show the paint
colour for each plot

_____

_____

_____

_____

_____

_____

_____

_____

_____

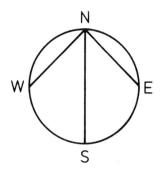

Figure 115   *Compass*

Task six

8 One of your employees is a consistently poor timekeeper and has also on occasions been absent for the whole day. When approached regarding the reasons for this conduct s/he replied: 'I find the work boring and can't really be bothered to get up in the morning'.

(i) State the procedure to be followed for terminating this person's employment; and

(ii) state the circumstances under which an employee may be instantly dismissed

Part three

Construction, the Environment and the Community

After working through this part of the book the student should be able to:

1 Interpret the need for conservation and improvement of the environment.

2 Indicate how buildings and construction may enhance or mar the environment.

3 State how the need for buildings changes with economic and social change.

4 Recognize and name the main types of historical buildings and relate their design to the social needs at the time of their construction.

5 Interpret simple aesthetic principles relating to the interior and exterior appearance of buildings.

6 State the social effects of building obsolescence and of methods of renewal and renovation.

7 Interpret the ways in which society controls building work through planning and public health law.

Building control

Society exercises control over the use of land, building activities and buildings through legislation made by, or with, the authority of parliament. The *three* main areas of this control are:

Planning permission
Building regulations
Health and safety controls

In brief, *planning permission* controls restrict the type and position of a building or development in relation to the environment, whereas the *building regulations* state how a building should be constructed to ensure safe and healthy accommodation and the conservation of energy. Both of these forms of control are administered by the relevant local authorities, to whom an application must normally be made prior to starting work. *Health and safety controls*, on the other hand, are concerned with the health and safety of building-site workers, visitors and the general public. These controls are administered by the Health and Safety Executive under the Health and Safety at Work Act 1974.

Note: Health and safety controls are considered in detail in Topic 11, Building Safety (p. 128).

Planning permission

All development is controlled by planning laws, which exist to control the use and development of land in order to obtain the greatest possible environmental advantages with the least inconvenience, both for the individual and society as a whole. The submission of a planning application provides the local authority and the general public with an opportunity to consider the development and decide whether or not it is in the general interest of the locality. The key word in planning is *development*. This means all building work, other operations such as the construction of a driveway, and a change of land or building use, such as running a business from your home.

The Town and Country Planning Act 1971 sets out certain categories of work which are not considered as development. These are: improvement works which only affect the interior of a dwelling; maintenance or improvement of roads carried out by the local highway authority; inspection or repair works to sewers, pipes and cables etc. carried out by the local authority or the statutory undertakings; use of land for agricultural or forestry purposes; use of land or buildings within the grounds of a dwelling for purposes directly relating to the enjoyment of the occupants of the dwelling.

Permitted developments

The Town and Country Planning Act also sets out under General Development Orders certain classes of development known as *permitted developments* where no planning approval is required as the Secretary of State for the Environment has already granted automatic permission for them. These include: limited extensions and certain alterations to dwellings; temporary uses of land; erection of boundary fences and walls within certain height limits.

Extensions

Extensions to detached and semi-detached domestic houses are classified as permitted developments providing they do not exceed $70\,m^3$ or 15% of the original volume of the house up to a maximum of $115\,m^3$. Terraced houses are restricted, however, to $50\,m^3$ or 10% of the original volume up to a maximum of $115\,m^3$. In all cases these extensions must not:

(i) project in front of the house if it faces a public highway (except small porches of $2\,m^2$ maximum floor area and less than 3-metres high);

(ii) cover more than 50% of the garden;

(iii) be higher than the house; and

(iv) be within 2 metres of the boundary if the extension is higher than 4 metres

Planning application

When Planning Permission is required, an application is made to the planning department of the relevant local authority. The main types of application are:

Outline planning permission
Full planning permission
Discharge of conditions attached to a previous application
Listed building consent
Consent to display advertisements

Outline planning permission

This enables the owner or prospective owner to obtain approval of the proposed development, in principle, without having to incur the costs involved with the preparation of full working drawings, thus leaving certain aspects of the development for later approval.

Full planning permission

After obtaining outline planning permission, and when full details of the development have been decided, an application for full planning permission can be made. Alternatively, an outline application can be dispensed with and full planning permission sought at the outset. An application for full permission must normally include four copies of a standard form and four copies of plans and drawings as follows (see Figure 116).

A plan must be provided, drawn to a scale of not less than 1:2500, which shows the site shaded in red and its relationship to adjacent properties.

Further drawings must be produced that give a clear picture of any new building as well as the existing features of the site including trees. These drawings, normally of a scale not less than 1:100 must clearly indicate the position of the proposed development within the site and the amount of floor space to be used for each purpose. In addition, the types and colours of materials for the external walls and roof should be indicated together with the proposed access to the site and the types of fence or wall surrounding the development.

After considering these details in light of the authorities' planning policies and their effect on the amenity of the surrounding area and also taking into consideration the views of neighbours, members of the public and public bodies, the planning committee can either:

Grant permission
Grant permission with certain conditions
Refuse permission

Where permission is refused or given conditionally the committee must give their reasons for the decision. Applicants can then modify the proposed development and re-submit their application, or appeal against the decision to the Secretary of State for the Environment.

Listed building consent

Certain buildings of historic or special architectural interest may be included in a list of buildings drawn up by the Secretary of State for the Environment. Buildings included in this list are protected by law. It is an offence to pull down, alter or extend a listed building unless authorized by *listed building consent*. Listed

TOWN AND COUNTRY PLANNING ACT 1971
APPLICATION FOR PERMISSION TO DEVELOP LAND

BRACKENDOWNS
BOROUGH COUNCIL

Building Control Dept
Council Buildings
Brackendowns
Bedfordshire
BR1 4AC

For office use only

Borough ref. _____

Registered no. _____

Date received _____

1 APPLICANT

AGENT (if any) to whom correspondence should be sent

Name _____

Name _____

Address _____

Address _____

_____ Tel. no. _____

_____ Tel. no. _____

2 PARTICULARS OF PROPOSED DEVELOPMENT

(a) Full address or location
of the land to which
this application relates and
site area (if known).

(b) Brief particulars of proposed
development including the
purpose(s) for which the land
and/or buildings are to be used.

(c) State whether applicant owns or
controls any adjoining land and
if so, give its location.

(d) State whether the proposal involves: State Yes or No

(i) New building(s) _____

If 'Yes' state gross floor area
of proposed building(s). m^2/sq ft*

If residential development,
state number of dwelling units
proposed and type if known,
e.g. houses, bungalows, flats.

(ii) Alterations _____

(iii) Change of use _____

(iv) Construction of a new } vehicular
access to a highway } pedestrian

(v) Alteration of an existing } vehicular
access to a highway } pedestrian

If 'Yes' state gross area of land
or building(s) affected by
proposed change of use (if
more than one use involved
state gross area of each use).

hectares/acres/m^2/sq ft*

*Please delete whichever inapplicable

3 PARTICULARS OF APPLICATION

State whether this application is for: State Yes or No

If 'Yes' delete any of the following which are not reserved
for subsequent approval

(i) Outline planning permission _____

(ii) Full planning permission _____

| 1 | siting | 3 | external appearance |
| 2 | design | 4 | means of access |

(iii) Renewal of a temporary
permission or permission for
retention of building or
continuance of use without
complying with a condition
subject to which planning
permission has been granted _____

If 'Yes' state the date and number of previous permission
and identify the particular condition (see General Notes)

Date

Number

The condition

(iv) Consideration under Section 72 only
(Industry)

Figure 116   *Planning application form*

building consent is required for any works which alter the style or character of a listed building either internally or externally. This includes any works which do not require planning permission and, as well as the listed building, it also includes any out-buildings, walls and railings etc. within the boundary.

Buildings of outstanding national importance are given the top listing, being classified as Grade I (about 65% of the total listed buildings receive this grade). Buildings of outstanding regional importance are given a Grade II★ classification (about 15% of the total). Buildings of ordinary regional importance are classified as Grade II. In total, about 500,000 buildings are listed.

Owners of listed buildings are required to preserve them in good order. If they fail to do so, the local authority may serve on the owner a *Repairs Notice*. This notice lists the repairs that the owner must carry out immediately; failure to do so can result in the local authority purchasing the building compulsorily, or carrying out the repairs themselves and recovering the costs from the owner. In certain cases owners of listed buildings may be eligible for special grants or loans from the local authority towards the costs of repairs.

Advertisement control

The display of advertisements such as shop signs, hoardings and banners etc. are controlled by town and country planning regulations. Certain advertisements are free of control and do not require the express approval of the local authority. Others such as illuminated advertisements and advertisements at, or above, first-floor level do generally require local authority approval.

The two main considerations taken into account when considering an advertisement application are *highway safety* and *amenity*. No advertisement will be permitted if, in the view of the local authority, it will distract drivers, be mistaken for a road sign, or spoil the appearance of a building or area. Like general planning decisions, in the event of a refusal there is right

of appeal to the Secretary of State for the Environment.

Enforcement of planning controls

Where work has been carried out without planning permission or when conditions attached to planning permission have not been complied with, the local authority has the power to serve an *Enforcement Notice*. This will state what has to be done to rectify the situation within a set time limit. If an Enforcement Notice is ignored, substantial fines can be imposed by subsequent court proceedings. In the case of listed buildings, the fine may be of an unlimited amount and or up to twelve months' imprisonment. Where an Enforcement Notice has been served, the local authority may, at its discretion, also serve a *Stop Notice*. Anyone served with an Enforcement or Stop Notice can appeal to the Secretary of State for the Environment.

Building regulations

Approval

The need for building regulations control arose at the time of the Industrial Revolution, when society and the economy was changing from being mainly agricultural to mainly industrial. Development at this time was very rapid but largely uncontrolled by local authorities and resulted in the appalling conditions of working-class housing. The Public Health Act of 1875 allowed local authorities to make local bye-laws to control the construction of new streets, the chimneys, the general layout of buildings and external space requirements. In addition, the Act also gave local authorities powers for closing down dwellings they deemed to be unfit for human habitation. In 1966 these local bye-laws were replaced by national Building Regulations which ensured that buildings were safe and healthy and that all building work was designed and implemented correctly. In 1984 a new Building Act was approved by parliament. The Building Regulations 1985 were made under this act and apply to all building work carried out in England and Wales including Inner London

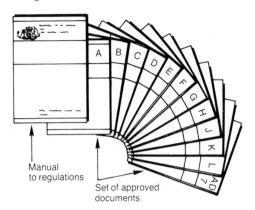

Figure 117 *Building regulations*

(previously building regulations control in inner London was carried out by District Surveyors under the London Building Acts).

Note: Similar controls and regulations exist for building work in Scotland and Northern Ireland.

The Building Regulations 1985 are supported by two additional documents (see Figure 117).

A manual to the Regulations
A set of approved documents

As these documents are outside the statutory instrument of law, they have been written in a clear technical style and contain illustrations rather than the quasi-legal language of the previous Regulations. The following approved documents are available:

Structure
Fire
Site preparation and resistance to moisture
Toxic substances
Sound
Ventilation
Hygiene
Drainage and waste disposal
Heat-producing appliances
Stairways, ramps and guards
Conservation of fuel and power
Materials and workmanship

Approved documents are intended to give practical guidance to ways of complying with the Regulations. When designing a building, you are free to use the solutions given in the approved documents or devise your own solutions providing you show that you meet the requirements of the Regulations. In addition, the Regulations also contain details of facilities for disabled people.

Application

Whenever anyone wishes to erect a new building, extend or alter an existing one, or change the use of an existing building, s/he will probably require building regulations approval, in addition to any planning-control applicable.

Certain classes of building are *exempted* from the regulations. In addition to Crown and educational buildings these include:

Class 1 Buildings controlled by other legislation, e.g. Explosives Acts; Nuclear Installations Act; Ancient Monuments and Archaeological Areas Act.

Class 2 Buildings not used by people, e.g. a detached building where people cannot, or do not, normally enter.

Class 3 Glasshouse and agricultural buildings.

Class 4 Temporary buildings and mobile homes (temporary buildings are defined as those which are intended to remain erected for less than 28 days).

Class 5 Ancillary buildings, e.g. temporary building-site accommodation and any building other than a dwelling used in connection with a mine or quarry.

Class 6 Small detached buildings, e.g. a detached building of up to $30\,m^2$ floor area which does not contain sleeping accommodation; a detached building of up to $30\,m^2$ floor area designed to shelter people from the effects of nuclear, chemical or conventional weapons.

Class 7 Extensions (of up to $30\,m^2$ floor area) e.g. the ground-floor extension to a building by the addition of a greenhouse, conservatory, porch, covered yard or covered way; a carport which is open on at least two sides.

BRACKENDOWNS BOROUGH COUNCIL
BUILDING CONTROL DEPARTMENT

The Building Act 1984
The Building Regulations 1985
The Building (Prescribed Fees) Regulations

FULL PLANS NOTICE

PART 1.   TO BE COMPLETED IN ALL CASES

a)   Name and Address of Owner

a)   MR. W.H. WHITEMAN, WHITEMAN ENTERPRISES,
ENGINEERING HOUSE, BEDFORD.

Telephone No.   0641293

b)   Name and Address of Agent, if any

b)   B.B.S. DESIGN, SARBIE HOUSE,
BRACKENDOWNS, BEDS.

Telephone No.   0581 423

c)   Address or location of the building to
which this notice relates

c)   PLOT 3, HILLTOP ROAD, BRACKENDOWNS,
BEDS.

d)   Description of the building work

d)   NEW DETACHED HOUSE AND GARAGE

e)   Present use of building

e)   NOT APPLICABLE

f)   Proposed use of building

f)   PRIVATE DWELLING

g)   Do you agree to the plans being passed
subject to conditions?

g)   YES / NO

h)   Is a new crossing over a footway required?

h)   YES / NO

PART 2.   TO BE COMPLETED IF AN UNVENTED HOT WATER STORAGE SYSTEM IS TO BE INSTALLED

a)   Name and Type of System

a)   NOT APPLICABLE

b)   Agreement Certificate Number

b)

c)   Name and Address of Installer

c)

PART 3.   BUILDING (PRESCRIBED FEES) REGULATIONS — COMPLETE 'a', 'b' or 'c' and 'd'

a)	New Dwellings:— (enter number)	i)	Number of dwellings to which this notice relates	**ONE**
		ii)	Number of dwellings with floor area over 64m²	**ONE**
		iii)	Total number of dwellings in 'multiple work scheme'	/
b)	Garage, Carport, or Domestic Extensions — (tick as appropriate)	i)	Detached garage/carport with floor area under 40m²	/
		ii)	One or more rooms in roof space	/
		iii)	Domestic extension with floor area less than 20m²	/
		iv)	Domestic extension with floor area 20–40m²	/
c)	All other building work or Material Changes of Use :—	i)	Total estimated cost of work to which notice relates	£29,000
		ii)	Aggregate total estimated cost of all buildings in 'multiple work scheme'	£ /
d)	Plan Fee calculated in accordance with the current Building (Prescribed Fees) Regulations:—	i)	Plan Fee	£ 39
		ii)	Plus VAT at current rate	£ 5.85p
		iii)	Total Enclosed	£ 44.85p

PART 4   DECLARATION

This notice and duplicate copies of the relevant plans and particulars in relation to the above mentioned building work, are deposited in accordance with Building Regulation 11(1)(b).

The Plan Fee shown above is enclosed and I acknowledge that the relevant Inspection Fee will, upon demand after the first inspection, be payable to the Council by the person by whom, or on whose behalf, the work is being carried out.

Date   2nd MARCH 1986   Signed   D. Paull.   Agent
                                                                                                          F.T.O.

Figure 118   *Building Regulations application form*

This notice, together with the Plan Fee and duplicate copies of the plans and particulars referred to below, should be forwarded to:—

Building Control Department
Council Buildings
Brackendowns
Bedfordshire
BR1 4AC

PLANS are required to a scale of not less than 1:1250 showing:—

a) the size and position of the building, or the building as extended, and its relationship to adjoining boundaries.

b) the boundaries of the gardens of the building, or the building as extended, and the size, position and use of every other building or proposed building.

c) the width and position of any street on, or within, the boundaries.

PLANS are also required to suitable scales and, where appropriate, PARTICULARS, to show that the work complies with the relevant Building Regulations:—

Part A — Structure
Part B — Fire
Part C — Site Preparation & Resistance to Moisture
Part D — Toxic Substances
Part E — Resistance to the Passage of Sound
Part F — Ventilation

Part G — Hygiene
Part H — Drainage & Waste Disposal
Part J — Heat Producing Appliances
Part K — Stairways, Ramps & Guards
Part L — Conservation of Fuel & Power

Schedule 2 — Facilities for Disabled People
Regulation 7 — Materials & Workmanship

PARTICULARS should also be provided:—

a) if Section 24 of the Building Act 1984 applies (i.e. provision of exits in theatres, restaurants, shops, clubs, schools and churches) the provisions to be made for the matters described in that section.

b) if Section 18 of the Building Act 1984 applies (i.e. building over public sewers) either the precautions to be taken in building over the sewer or proposals for its diversion. (see note below)

PLEASE NOTE:—

1. A MAP OF PUBLIC SEWERS is available for inspection by the public in the Council's Engineers department. If you are proposing to erect or extend a building it is recommended that, before preparing or depositing plans, you check that sewers are available and will not be built over, unless prior agreement has been reached with the Engineer with regard to the precautions to be taken or for diversion of the sewer.

2. NEW CONNECTIONS TO PUBLIC SEWERS require a separate consent under Section 34 of the Public Health Act 1936. Details are available from the Council's Engineer.

3. TOWN & COUNTRY PLANNING PERMISSION may be required for your proposals. If in doubt, please check with the Council's Planning Department.

Figure 118 continued

When building regulations approval *is required*, the building-control section of the relevant local authority must be notified of your intentions by one of the following three methods:

Deposit full plans
Issue a Building Notice
Appoint an Approved Inspector

Full plans
Application using the full-plans method (see Figure 118) can be made by depositing (in duplicate) full plans of the proposed works. These shall consist of:

1 A statement that the plans are deposited in accordance with the Building Regulations 1985.
2 A full description of the proposed work (specification).
3 Details of the surrounding area (block plan).
4 The intended use of the proposed building.
5 Drawings to a scale of not less than 1:1250 showing the size and position of the building, its boundaries and relationship to adjoining boundaries (site plan and general location plans).
6 The number of storeys in the building.
7 The provision made for drainage.
8 Details of any cavity-wall insulation and its installer.
9 Details of any unvented hot-water system.
10 Any other details or plans if required to show that the work will comply with the regulations.

These plans and details will be examined to see if they comply with the regulations; a decision will be made within five weeks or two months if you agree to an extension of time. The plans may be *rejected* on any of the following grounds:

1 The plans show a contravention of the regulations.
2 The plans are defective (they fail to show compliance with the regulations).
3 They contravene or show insufficient detail with regards to one of the local authority's

functions under the Building Act (e.g. drainage, water supply, public buildings and local legislation).

Where an application is refused or the applicant and the local authority are in dispute, there is an appeals procedure to the Secretary of State for the Environment.

Note: The local authority has the power to relax or dispense with certain requirements of the Building Regulations.

Building notice
Application using the Building Notice method can be made by depositing a Building Notice and limited accompanying information (e.g. specification, block plan, site plan and general location plans). In addition, the local authority may request further information as the work proceeds, in order to show compliance of specific items which cannot be inspected on site (e.g. structural calculations, material specifications etc.).

Note: You cannot use the Building Notice method when erecting shops or offices.

Approved Inspector
Application using the Approved Inspector method can be made by you and the inspector jointly, by depositing an initial notice, limited plans and evidence of their insurance cover to the local authority. The local authority must accept or reject this initial notice within ten working days. Once accepted, their powers to enforce the Regulations are suspended and the Approved Inspector will carry out the building-control function and issue a final certificate to you and the local authority when the work has been completed satisfactorily.

Inspection of building work
When either the full plans method or the Building Notice method has been adopted, the local authority's Building Control Officer will inspect the work as it proceeds. The builder

must give the local authority written notice of the following building stages (this notice need not be in writing if the local authority agrees):

1 At least 48 hours before the commencement of work.
2 At least 24 hours before the covering up of any excavation for a foundation, any foundation, any damp-proof course or any concrete or other material laid over a site.
3 At least 24 hours before haunching or covering up any drain.
4 Not more than seven days after laying, concreting or backfilling a drain.
5 Not more than seven days after completion of building work.

Where builders fail to notify the local authority of any stage as required, the local authority has the power to require them to 'open up' or 'pull down' part of the work at a later date to enable inspection. After inspection by the Building Control Officer, the local authority may require modifications or additional work to be carried out in order to comply with the Regulations.

Where an Approved Inspector has been appointed s/he will be responsible for inspecting the work as it proceeds. The Inspector may also require the builder to notify commencement and/or particular stages of building work.

The local authority will charge a set fee for considering an application and inspecting the work as it proceeds. If an Approved Inspector is appointed, s/he will negotiate the fee with you.

Self-assessment questions

Question   *Your answer*

1 Briefly describe the purpose of the following legislation:
  (i) Planning permission
  (ii) Building Regulations

_____

_____

_____

_____

2 Name *three* operations that constitute in planning terms, 'development'

_____

_____

_____

_____

3 Explain the meaning of:
  (i) Outline planning permission; and
  (ii) full planning permission

_____

_____

_____

_____

4 State the *three* methods of notifying a local authority of your intention to build

_____

_____

_____

_____

5 Name *three* of the building
   stages that local authorities
   must be given notice of when
   they are responsible for the
   inspection of building work

6 Two of the following extensions to buildings are *exempted*
   from the need to comply with
   the Building Regulations:
   1 Conservatory
   2 Kitchen
   3 Bathroom
   4 Porch
   Which are they?
   (a) 1 and 2
   (b) 2 and 3
   (c) 3 and 4
   (d) 4 and 1?

   7 Briefly explain what consti-
     tutes a listed building

Building and the environment

In our densely-populated country, where land is strictly limited, there are many competing and often conflicting uses for land that have to be resolved. Therefore it is essential to ensure that the best possible use is made of this scarce resource for the social and economic well-being of society as a whole. It is necessary to ensure that there is adequate provision of essential facilities in areas like schools, health centres and recreational spaces etc. In certain circumstances, in order to provide these essential facilities it may be necessary to resist the more profitable use of land for commercial, industrial or housing purposes.

As well as land use, the general appearance of the environment is equally important and needs to be controlled, in order to prevent badly designed buildings or other development which may mar instead of enhance the environment. Clearly, the design and quality of the environment is a matter of individual opinion, as what is good taste or acceptable to one person may be the complete opposite to another. But poorly designed or badly sited developments can make life very unpleasant for those living or working in the vicinity. We cannot solve all the problems created in the past, but to improve the quality of life we must have controls to prevent new problems occurring in the future. These controls are exercised through a national system of environmental planning. The responsibilities of this system are split into *three* distinct areas.

National government

The Secretary of State for the Environment and the government department are responsible for the general organization of the planning system on a national basis. They approve *structure plans*, deal with major planning applications and handle appeals made against the decision of local authorities.

County council

The county council is responsible for preparing, updating and submitting the structure plan for approval to the Secretary of State for the Environment. This plan provides a general policy framework for future development within the whole of the county. In addition, it has a town and country planning role for applications involving minerals and waste disposal and its own developments including roads and schools etc.

Borough council

The |borough| council is responsible for interpreting the structure plan policies in more detail at local level and producing *local plans*. In addition, it is responsible for the majority of town and country planning applications, conservation and tree preservation.

Structure plans

The structure plan is basically a statement of a county's planning policy. It consists of a written statement, supported by various diagrams, which sets out the important general proposals for the area and provides justification for them. The main items covered in the plan are population, employment, resources, housing, industry, commerce, transportation, shopping, education, social and community services, recreation and leisure, conservation, utility services and minerals.

Local plans

The local plans consist basically of a proposals map and a written statement, on how the area should develop over the next ten years. They should develop the general policies and proposals of the structure plan into specific policies and proposals related to precisely defined areas of land. Therefore it provides the detailed basis for making decisions on applications for planning

permission and also general guidance to developers and other concerned parties.

Figure 119 shows a typical local plan. Approximately 3000 people live in this area which also provides 3600 jobs mainly in small manufacturing firms of less than 50 employees. This area consists almost entirely of buildings constructed in the Victorian period. Therefore it has a number of problems which are typically associated with older housing neighbourhoods in inner-city areas, e.g. a lack of open space; a mixture of houses and factories; intrusive traffic; on-street parking; and a large number of houses in poor condition.

The plan deals with these problems by the following:

Identifying the area where employment use is predominant and well established. Designating this area the main employment area and allowing in this area a gradual change of use away from housing to provide new employment opportunities.

Concentration will be made on improving housing conditions and discouraging employment uses outside the main employment area.

Conservation

Within the ever-changing society in which we live there is an increasing need to conserve things of beauty. These include parts of buildings, individual buildings, whole areas, trees, open spaces, landmarks and the atmosphere.

Local authorities have a duty to promote and secure the conservation of the environment within their own boundaries. These duties are important as they are intended to protect cherished aspects of an area's existing character from insensitive changes, and promote sympathetically styled new development. In practice, successful conservation of the environment relies on cooperation between the local authority, property owners and residents.

Local authorities can act directly to improve public areas such as roads, open spaces and their own buildings etc., in addition to their powers in controlling new development. Property owners

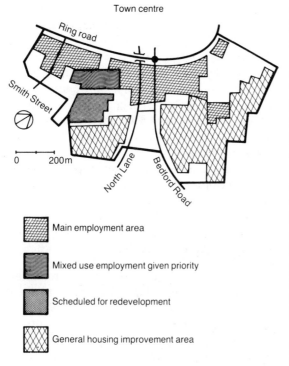

Main employment area

Mixed use employment given priority

Scheduled for redevelopment

General housing improvement area

Figure 119   *Local plan*

and individual residents have an equal role to play since the pride they take in their area and the decisions they make concerning the treatment of their own building, gardens and other areas, affect the appearance of the neighbourhood as a whole.

Shown in Figure 120 is an example of insensitive change to one of a pair of semi-detached houses. All the original features and materials have been retained in the house on the left-hand side, whereas the one on the right-hand side has had its window openings altered, its face brickwork rendered over, its balustrading removed and its ornamental ridge tiles replaced, completely changing the character of the property.

When extending existing property, the aim should be to blend the extension into the character of the existing building and not look as though it is an after-thought, which has been added on. Figure 121 shows two pairs of semi-detached houses. The first (a) shows how extensions can look out of place. The dormer roof extension severely alters the roof line and the flat roof to the additional room over the garage looks added on. A proposed development of this type could cause planning problems, neighbour disputes as well as marring the environment. A more pleasing solution is

(A) Out of place extension

(B) A blending extension

Figure 121　*Extensions to existing property*

illustrated in (b), where the extension blends with the existing. In cases where roof extensions are required, dormer windows are far more acceptable at the rear rather than the front of properties.

Encouragement is given to local authorities to define and declare *conservation areas*. These are areas of outstanding character and quality where it is desirable to preserve and enhance appearance and control new development. The principal aim is to encourage rehabilitation or refurbishment of existing buildings (residential, commercial and industrial) rather than comprehensive redevelopment which splits communities.

Buildings in conservation areas are protected from demolition or alteration unless the local authority previously grants permission.

There is financial assistance available to property owners for improvements and repairs to residential property in both conservation and general residential areas. This assistance is available in the form of a Housing Renovation Grant/Loan from the local authority.

Tree preservation

Trees are an essential part of our environment, both in the town and country areas. Many individual trees or groups of trees are protected

Figure 120　*Example of insensitive change*

by Tree Preservation Orders (TPOs) issued by the local authority. Their purpose is to protect trees. Their owner is required to obtain the local authorities approval to lop, top, prune or fell a protected tree. Felling or damaging a protected tree without prior consent can result in prosecution. Where approval to fell is granted, the owner is normally required to plant a suitable replacement in the same position.

The majority of trees in conservation areas are automatically protected by TPOs and anyone wishing to lop, top, prune or fell a tree in such an area must give the local authority six weeks' notice of their intent.

Aesthetic design principles

Aesthetics is concerned with the appearance or 'beauty' of an item and is thus an individual opinion. The aesthetics of architecture is the province of the architect who has a sensitive, trained eye and can consider the complexities of *balance, unity and shape, texture* and *colour* to produce a design that will have the desired effect.

Balance

Balance is a major factor in the aesthetic appearance of a building. One essential feature of a balanced design is a focal point, on which the eye will rest naturally. This is often arranged to be the main entrance. Visual balance and physical balance work in similar ways, the focal point in visual balance being the equivalent of the fulcrum in physical balance, the purpose of both being to obtain equilibrium (balance). Two identical bricks placed on a beam at an equal distance from the fulcrum will produce a balance that is symmetrical, whereas a brick and a bag of cement will have to be placed at different distances from the fulcrum to obtain a balance; this is known as asymmertical balance. Figure 122 illustrates this principle and applies it to buildings.

In buildings with symmetrical balance, either side of the focal point must be an identical mirror image, whilst in asymmetrical balance they are not. In general, symmetrical designs give a formal effect (classical architecture), while asymmetrical designs are more relaxed (modern architecture).

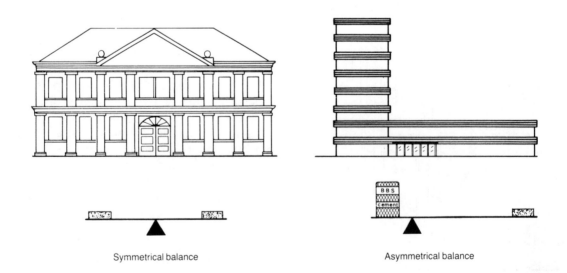

Symmetrical balance   Asymmetrical balance

Figure 122   *Balance*

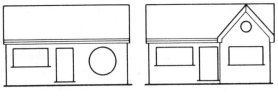

(A) Disunity   (B) Unity

Figure 123   *Unity and disunity*

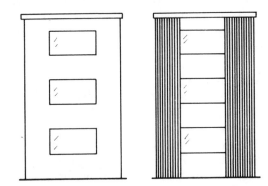

Figure 124   *Texture*

Figure 125   *Overuse of contrast*

Unity and shape

Unity and shape are other important factors in the aesthetic appearance of a building. Figure 123 illustrates two examples of design using contrasting shapes, in (a) neither of the shapes dominate resulting in disunity, whereas in (b) because one of the shapes is larger, it dominates and unity is therefore achieved.

Texture

Texture can be used to great advantage in enhancing the appearance of a building. Texture is the degree of surface finish used, e.g. how smooth or rough are surfaces. The appearance of buildings can be improved by the inclusion of contrasting texture as shown in Figure 124.

Colour

The use of contrasting colours like texture can be used to great advantage in enhancing the appearance of a building. Many building materials have their own natural distinctive colourings; with others it is possible to apply colour using paint and wallpaper etc., to achieve the desired contrast.

Although the use of contrasting colours and textures can enhance the appearance of a building, care is needed when using them as too much contrast will mar its appearance resulting in an eyesore (see Figure 125).

Glossary of environmental terms

Built environment   This consists of man-made constructions which are required to fulfil society's needs and consists of accommodation and facilities for living, working, recreation, religious activities, storage and transport.

City   A large or important *Town* which is created a city by the granting of a charter. Most cathedral towns are cities, e.g. Coventry. The business centre or original area of a large town is called the city, e.g. The City of London.

Conservation   Environmental conservation is concerned with the maintenance of the *Environment* in its entirety. This involves maintaining the cherished aspects of our heritage. e.g. buildings, trees, open spaces, landmarks and the atmosphere.

Conurbation   A merging of a group of *Towns* and *Villages* into one large, built-up *Urban* area.

Density   The system of measuring the amount of housing (accommodation density) or the number of people (population density) in a specific area of land. Detached housing does not normally exceed 20 dwellings per hectare (10,000 m^2). Semi-detached 30, and terraced 50. High-rise housing in the form of flats or maisonettes is required to achieve density levels above these. In general, as density increases problems associated with noise, loss of privacy, mental stress and vandalism emerge.

Derelict Land or buildings that have been damaged by serious neglect or other processes, which in their existing state are unsightly and incapable of use without treatment.

Environment Our physical surroundings, including people, buildings, structures, land, water, atmosphere, climate, sound, smell and taste.

Green belt Areas of open land around *Urban* areas to prevent further expansion. They are kept open by severe and permanent planning restrictions.

Obsolescence Items or buildings etc. that become out of date or practice and fall into disuse.

Pollution Any direct or indirect alteration of the *Environment*, hazardous or potentially hazardous to health, safety and welfare of any living species.

Preservation The keeping in existence unchanged, natural resources and buildings etc. which have been inherited from the past.

Redevelopment To demolish the existing buildings in an area, replan it and then rebuild.

Refurbishment To bring an existing building up to standard or make it suitable for a new use by *Renovation*, re-equipping or restoring it.

Rehabilitation *Slum* areas and buildings brought up to an acceptable living standard.

Renovation Bringing an existing building back to its former or original condition.

Restoration The same as *Renovation*.

Rural In the country.

Slum An overcrowded, dirty, neglected, unhygienic building or area normally inhabited by poor people.

Suburb A residential area situated on the outskirts of a *Town* or *City*. Hence suburban and suburbia.

Town A large collection of dwellings bigger than a *Village* but not created a *City*.

Urban A *Town* or *City* area.

Urbanization The process of change from a *Rural* to an *Urban* area.

Village A small collection of dwellings with a church in a *Rural* area.

Zoning A system of planning land use based on boundaries, inside which land can only be used for a specified use, e.g. agriculture, dwellings, industry or recreation etc.

Self-assessment questions

Question

Your answer

1 State the responsibilities of the national government in the system of environmental planning

2 Briefly describe the purpose of our national system of environmental planning

3 Distinguish between structure plans and local plans and state who is responsible for preparing them

_____

4 Name and state the purpose of a TPO

_____

5 Define the following environmental terms:
   (i)   Green belt
   (ii) Refurbishment
   (iii) Suburban

_____

6 Describe the methods by which a local authority can promote the conservation of the environment

_____

7 Define and distinguish between symmetrical and asymmetrical design

_____

The history of building – from Stone Age to Gothic

The dates and titles of the various building styles or architectural periods shown in Table 8 have been given to them by historians. Although they are a simple classification, it must be remembered that often the styles overlap the periods, there being a form of transition where style developed from its predecessors as social conditions and influences changed.

Table 8 **The historical styles of building – I**

Date	Period/style	Title	Features
Up to AD 43	Stone Age Bronze Age Iron Age	Prehistoric	Caves, tents, huts, stone huts, encampments, pit dwellings, wattle and daub huts, lake villages, stone monuments
AD 43–410		Roman	Engineering skills, central heating, plumbing, system of roads, mosaic floors, use of bricks, concrete and glass
410–1066 1066–1200	Anglo-Saxon Anglo-Norman	Romanesque	Early heathenism, timber-frame houses, 'cotes' and 'halls', churches, cathedrals, the feudal system, manor houses, castles
1200–1300 1300–1400 1400–1500	Early English Decorated Perpendicular	Gothic	Pointed arches, flying buttresses, tracery, hammer-beam roofs, spires, vaulting, strong Christianity, great churches, Black Death

Prehistoric

The story of building started many thousands of years before the Roman conquest, in a time which is called *Prehistoric*.

Stone Age (Figure 126)

Our earliest ancestors, the Old Stone Age people (Paleolithic) were hunters who moved about from place to place in search of food and

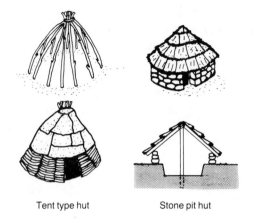

Tent type hut   Stone pit hut

Figure 126   *Stone Age huts*

thus built no permanent homes. Each night they would require shelter from wild animals and the weather. These were probably hollow dug-outs in the earth and covered with branches, turf and vegetation or animal skins to form a roof.

With the coming of the Great Ice Age the winters became extremely cold. Many of the animals and humans travelled south towards warmer climates, but some remained and took to living in caves for the extra protection.

By about 10,000 years BC, during the Middle Stone Age (Mesolithic), the weather was becoming warmer, the Polar ice caps melted. Britain became an island in about 8,000 BC. During this time the Red Indian type tent structure was common, consisting of long poles driven into the ground to form circular frameworks which were tied together at their tops. This framework was filled in with woven branches and reeds and covered with vegetation, wet clay or animal skins. Fires were lit outside the entrance of these tents in order to frighten off wild animals at night, provide heat and cook animal flesh.

By the coming of the New Stone Age (Neolithic) 3,000 BC, people were already keeping flocks of animals and living in fenced encampments for safety as well as companionship. They also began to farm the land and grow crops.

These Neolithic farmers constructed circular stone huts. A large straight pole in the centre of the hut supported the branch framework which was covered with turf. The interior height of the hut was increased by digging out the earth and lowering the floor level by up to a metre. These *pit dwellings*, as they were known, provided more comfort and were free of draughts.

In areas where there was no stone to make the walls, the farmers built *wattle* and *daub* huts. These consisted of a circular ring of wooden posts forming the wall framework. From these, poles were spanned up to the taller post in the middle. Onto this framework, the builders wove a reed basket-work called wattle. A mixture of wet mud and dung was daubed (plastered) over the wattle to protect the inside of the hut from the wind and rain.

Huts were built in clusters (villages) and surrounded by a fence and a ditch for protection. The people living in each cluster were known as a tribe, under the leadership of a tribal chief.

During the Neolithic Age, huge stone monuments were erected, e.g. Stonehenge and Avebury. These are in the main near to long burrows (mass burial places) which indicate that they have some form of religious significance.

Bronze and Iron Ages (Figure 127)

During the Bronze Age (1800–500 BC) and the Iron Age (500 BC–AD 43), people continued to live in tribes. Iron Age people had the use of more sophisticated tools; they were able to fell larger trees and thus make larger buildings.

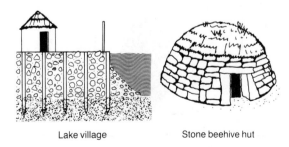

Lake village   Stone beehive hut

Figure 127   *Bronze and Iron Age huts*

As many of these tribes were constantly warring it became necessary to find new ways of protecting their homes and possessions. Some tribes built hill forts on high land surrounded by single or multiple earth banks, whilst others built their homes on lakes or marshes.

One famous lake village called Glastonbury was built on a man-made island. Hundreds of tree trunks were driven into the mud to form a foundation; earth and stones were piled into the enclosed area to form platforms on which the wattle and daub huts were built. The roofs of the huts were made of reeds woven into a thatch.

In areas where stone was plentiful, beehive huts of dry-stone walls were constructed; the stone roof was weathered with turf. Inside, large stones were used as furniture.

Roman (Figure 128)

The Romans invaded Britain in AD 43 and quickly colonized much of lowland Britain, although the tribes in present-day Scotland, Wales and Cornwall were largely unaffected by Roman rule. In order to keep the Scottish tribes

Figure 128   *Roman temples*

at bay, Hadrian's Wall was built to wall off Scotland. This is about 117 km long, 4–5 m high and 3 m wide. Forts were built at intervals along the wall itself and a deep trench was dug on its north side.

The Romans brought with them a highly developed system of building which they adapted to suit the local conditions and material resources. Roads were quickly constructed all over the country to enable quick and efficient troop movement. Many walled towns were built on a regular grid pattern. These had well-built houses, shops, baths, temples, arenas, town halls and in addition the Romans organized an efficient water supply, a drainage system and paved streets.

Their buildings were constructed of stone, bricks and mortar, finished with plaster. The roofs were of tile or stone slates. The floors were hollow to enable warm air from a furnace to circulate underneath them. This also extended to the walls which included hollow sections to allow the heat to rise inside them. Thousands of small coloured stones were set in cement to form intricate patterns and pictures on the floors (mosaic). Their windows were glazed with a thick glass; kitchens had a brick or stone oven, the interiors were comfortably furnished and contained elegant pottery and bronze work. These buildings were intended to be occupied by Roman officials and merchants, although wealthy Britions soon began to seek the extra comfort and copy them. Slaves in towns lived in blocks of flats, or tenements called *insular*.

Country houses or villas were built in the large farming estates. They usually had brick or concrete walls with an upper story consisting of a timber, frame filled in with wattle. Unlike the Britons' wattle which was daubed with clay, the Romans used a fine smooth plaster which they were able to colour to provide a more decorative finish. Like the town houses the villas had glazed windows, central heating, mosaic floors and furniture. The peasants who worked the land lived much the same as they had done for centuries before in wattle and daub huts or pit dwellings.

Romanesque

Romanesque is the name given to the period between the break up of the Roman Empire and the coming of the Gothic era. The Romans who abandoned Briton in AD 410 to defend Rome from the Goths, left it open to attack; it was subsequently invaded by the Barbarian hoardes who burned, ransacked and pillaged the towns and villas, destroying much of the high standard of Roman civilization.

Anglo-Saxon

The Angles, Saxons and Jutes who invaded from across the North Sea were fighters and farmers who were neither civilized or used to life in towns. They made little attempt to live in the Roman buildings which fell into decay, or were broken up for use as building materials. Instead, they cleared sites in the forests to build their simple timber-framed homes.

Cotes and Halls (Figure 129)

The Saxons, being a sea-faring nation, applied their boat-building skills to the construction of houses. Their early timber-frame dwellings resembled inverted boat hulls. They would take two curved tree trunks and split them down the middle to make the pointed arch end-frames known as *crucks*. The two end-frames were joined at their apex by a ridge pole; this often needed a centre post for support. This framework of the early cruck houses was covered in with wattle and daub, and thatch or turf. Later upright side walls were developed by the use of tie beams, wall plates and vertical wall posts. The spaces between the posts, which were filled with wattle and daub, are known as *pans*. Thus the method is known as *post and pan work*. The central post supporting the ridge restricted the internal space and was replaced by a short 'king post' resting on a central tie beam. Rafters were laid from the wall plates to the ridge and weathered with thatch.

Wind holes, later to become known as windows, were made in the pans on the prevailing wind side of the house to give a good draught to the central fire and so gave rise to the term *window pane*.

Early entrance doorways were covered by simply hanging a length of animal skin across the opening. Later solid doors were made from vertical planks battened together with cross-pieces and pivot-hung using metal or wooden pins.

The chief's house or 'hall' was the largest in a village. In addition to the chief and his family, it also housed his warriors, slaves and oxen (a team of four used for ploughing). The peasants lived in tiny cotes constructed in the same way but much smaller.

Upper storeys were later constructed over the cruck halls by laying large planks to span across the wall plates. Access was provided by a simple internal ladder or an external staircase.

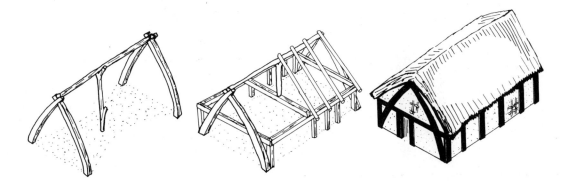

Figure 129   *Cruck frame houses*

Figure 130   *Saxon church tower (Earls Barton)*

Churches (Figures 130 and 131)

By about AD 600, Christianity had returned to England. Saxon churches, their first stone buildings, were noticeably small by later standards. As they were inexperienced in working with the material and had difficulties roofing over wide spans, their churches consisted of a series of rooms linked together by narrow semi-circular headed doorways. The entrance doorways were also semi-circular headed. Windows were small with semi-circular or triangular heads and wide internally-splayed reveals. Later, windows were grouped using stone balluster shafts to support the wall above. As the art of glass-making had been lost with the withdrawal of the Romans, timber shutters were used for protection from the weather.

Towers were very popular, and being the strongest part of the church it is often the only feature surviving to the present day. In addition to forming part of the body of the church, they also made excellent watch towers.

The corner stones (*quoins*) of the church and tower were strengthened by using what is termed 'long and short work'. This is alternate long vertical stones laid on top of flat horizontal slabs, the remainder of the wall being infilled with random stone. The external face of the walls was often decorated by letting in strips of stone into the wall face to form Pilaster strips, lattice work and blind arcading.

Normans

After the Normans conquered England in 1066, William 'The Conqueror' (Duke of Normandy) was pronounced King William of England. He went on to develop the Feudal System: all land became the property of the king. It was divided up between his barons, each being required to build a castle. The barons in turn gave lands (estates) to their knights who built manor houses. Along with each estate went unpaid serfs (mainly captured Saxons) who were bound to farm their masters' estate in return for protection and security. The serfs continued to live in simple wattle and daub cotes grouped around the castles and manor houses.

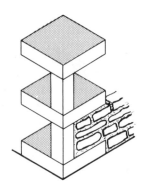

Figure 131   *Long and short Saxon corners*

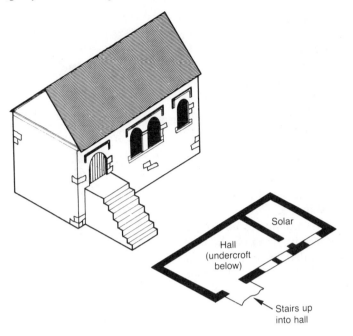

Figure 132 *Norman stone-built manor*

Manor houses (Figure 132)

At first Norman manor houses were basically cruck frame halls. Length was often increased through additional crucks, forming two (or more) bay long halls. The distance between crucks, about 5 metres, was called a *bay* which became a standard unit of land measurement variably called a *rod*, *pole* or *perch*. Halls could also be increased in width by extending the roof and walls past the line of the crucks, creating an aisle, known as an *outshut*.

Early stone-built manor houses were constructed with the hall at first-floor level, approached by external stairs. The ground-floor room known as the *undercroft* was used mainly for storage. Later, many manors had the hall situated on the ground floor. An upstairs room called a *solar* or *withdrawing room* (later shortened to *drawing room*) was added at one end of the hall. This gave the lord and his family privacy to withdraw and sleep. Access to the solar was provided either internally by a staircase or ladder, or externally by a staircase leading up to an oriel platform (a landing

projecting from an upper doorway). The under solar space (undercroft) was again often used for storage. A raised dias (platform) was normally provided at one end of the hall on which the lord, family and guests could dine separate from the rest of the household.

Castles (Figure 133)

The first Norman castles were timber structures built on the *motte and bailey* principle. This consisted of a timber tower built on top of a man-made mound of earth (motte) with a

Figure 133 *Norman motte and bailey castle*

timber-fenced courtyard surrounding it, called a bailey. The forming of the motte also created a defensive ditch or *moat* around the castle.

By the mid-12th Century, stone keep and bailey castles were being built. Keeps were massive stone towers normally four storey's high. These were not usually built on mottes because of foundation problems associated with their great weight on 'made-up' ground. Keeps, also called *donjons*, normally contained storage cellars, a chapel, kitchen, armoury, great hall and a solar. Windows were small and could be closed with wooden shutters. Fires were now placed against the wall, and smoke allowed to escape up a shaft built into it. Washing and toilet facilities were now included in an area of the solar called a *garderobe*. Access to the upper floor was via a solid stone spiral staircase.

Churches

The first Norman churches in England were actually constructed some years before the Norman invasion, by builders sent over from France, since there were close connections between the Saxon nobles and the Norman ruling house. The distinctive features of their buildings are massive thick walls, large rounded columns, semi-circular headed arches, vaulting and squat, square towers. The walls and columns were made from two skins of smooth cut stone, filled in with rubble, as illustrated in Figure 134.

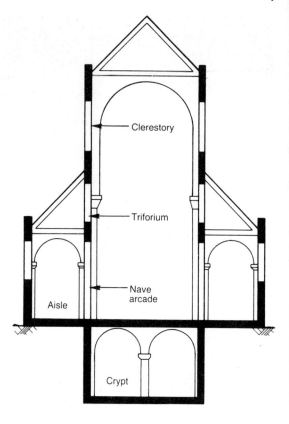

Figure 135 *Section through a church*

The great internal height of churches, which was intended to overwhelm worshippers, was achieved by the use of three storeys, a nave arcade (arches supported on pillars), a triforium (area under aisle roof) and a clerestory (the row of windows above the nave) (see Figure 135).

Windows were incorporated in the clerestory to light the nave or centre of the church. These were normally semi-circular headed, flanked by blind arcading (an arcade attached to a wall face for decoration). During the later Norman rule, they imported glass from Europe for use in stained-glass church windows and important houses.

Doorways were deeply recessed with a number of semi-circular arches supported on columns, each being decorated with carved mouldings, as shown in Figure 136. Underground crypts or cellars were floored-over, using stone

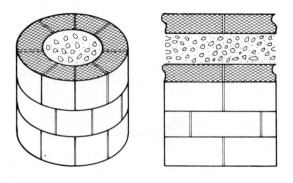

Figure 134 *Norman column and wall construction*

Figure 136   *Norman church doorway*

Early roofs consisted of timber trusses boarded on the underside to create a ceiling; later, with the development of ribbed vaults (a vault with reinforcing ribs across the bay to carry the stones or panels in between) stone roofs were used. This normally consisted of inner stone vaults with a steeply pitched timber roof on top to support the weathering material.

Gothic

The Gothic period in England arrived just as the Norman nobles must have considered themselves as 'English'. The Crusades of the 12th Century had enabled them to learn much about European architecture; this they interpreted into an English style. The term Gothic, meaning 'barbarous', was given to this period in the 18th Century by followers of 'civilized' Classical architecture, in order to distinguish it from what they called 'barbaric' English ('pointed') architecture.

Churches (Figure 138)

The main features of this period can be seen in church architecture: the general introduction of the pointed arch, ribbed vaults and buttresses.

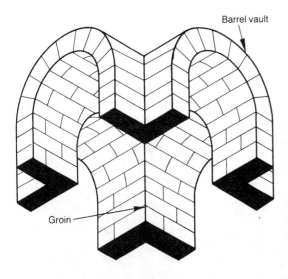

Figure 137   *Intersecting groined vault*

vaults. The simplest type of vault is a *barrel vault* which is simply a tunnel; where two barrel vaults intersect at right angles, a *cross-groined vault* is produced. The Normans omitted the barrels and used just the intersecting groined vaults supported on columns for their crypts (Figure 137).

Figure 138   *Flying buttresses*

The use of the pointed arch and ribbed vaults made it possible to use much thinner walls and slender columns as they transferred their loads to specific points. The outward pressure of the vaults was carried down by external buttresses (short cross-walls to take the thrust along their length). In large churches that contained a clerestory to light the nave, the height of the buttresses was raised so that a half-arch could be sprung over the aisle roof to transfer the thrust of the upper vaults. These *flying buttresses*, as they are known, became a marked external engineering feature.

Vaults became progressively more elaborate with the addition of extra ribs forming web-like patterns; rib junctions were often decorated with finely-carved bosses or knobs. Vaulting reached the height of refinement by the **perpendicular period**, with the *fan vault* named after its fan-like springing of ribs, and finally its variant the *pendant vault* with its ornamental suspended terminals.

Windows were incorporated in the bays between the buttresses. These were typically tall with a pointed arch at the top known as *lancet*

windows. Later these lancets were grouped together in two's and three's. Dripstones were built over the windows forming a hood, which prevented rain from running over them, from

Lancet   Grouped lancet
with plate tracery

EARLY ENGLISH

Figure 139   *Window frames*   Decorated   Perpendicular

Figure 140 *Pointed gothic-style doorway*

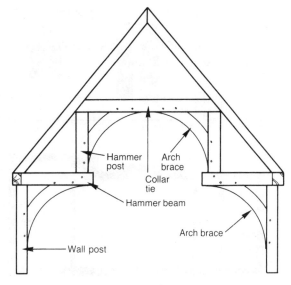

Figure 141 *Hammerbean roof*

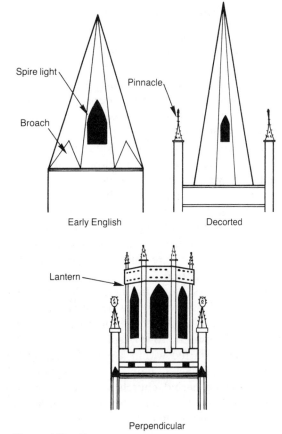

Figure 142 *Towers*

the walls above, and onto the window. The space created between the windows and the dripstone (called the *spandrel*) was pierced with circular trefoil or quatrefoil holes. (Trefoil and quatrefoil are patterns based on three or four foils, or parts of, a circle.) Thus the earliest forms of tracery called *plate tracery* were created. In the **decorated period**, true window tracery is introduced consisting of thin curved stone members supported by vertical stone mullions. This developed from trefoils and quatrefoils to *ogee* forms (convex and concave curves) through to flowing organic patterns. In the perpendicular period, windows became larger, filling the entire wall space between deep buttresses. These large windows, often with a flatter curvature arch, were sub-divided up with mullions and transoms into a rectangular network of glazed panels (see Figure 139).

Doorways (Figure 140) were often similar to Norman, but instead of the semi-circular arch, they were topped with a pointed arch; this got flatter with time and by the end of the perpendicular period, the flat four-centred arch was common. This was finished by a square

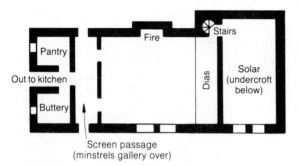

Figure 143 *Gothic stone-built manor house*

dripstone over them, and the spandrels filled with coats of arms or sculptures.

Early timber roofs over the top of stone-vaulted buildings were fairly steeply pitched and covered with stone tiles, slates or timber shingles. Later, much lower pitches were used and sheet lead became a popular covering. Roofs that were open from below in unvaulted buildings were decorated by woodcarvers. The finest examples appear in the perpendicular period with the hammerbeam roofs, which were richly decorated with fine carvings (see Figure 141). Richly carved timber screens, canopies and bench ends are also features of the perpendicular period.

Early towers were finished with stone or timber spires. Often spires were octagonal with *broaches*, making the transition to the square tower. Decorated tower spires were more slender and started within a parapet decorated with angle pinnacles. Few spires were built in perpendicular-period churches; instead towers were battlemented and topped with either a crown- or lantern-like structure (see Figure 142).

Manor houses (Figure 143)

Manor houses continued on much the same lines as their Norman predecessors, the hall being its major focal point. The solar was still placed at one end of the hall, with its undercroft store rooms. At the other end, a pantry (foodstore) and buttery (wine store) were added, their entrances being concealed by screens. The screens area which formed the entrance passage was often floored over to create a minstrels' gallery overlooking the hall. The kitchen was normally built in the courtyard separate from the hall, although later this was joined on and reached through the screens passage.

The stone walls were sometimes plastered with a mixture of powdered limestone and water strengthened with straw or animal hair. In wealthier homes, they could have been lined with timber panelling or covered with woven tapestries.

In common with churches, the windows were topped with pointed arches. Glass was very costly and only available in small pieces; these had to be joined together with lead strips to make a whole window pane or light. They were therefore known as *leaded light windows*. The lower part of the window was often hung on hinges, opening like a door and called a *casement*.

Roofs were formed using timber trusses, purlins and rafters and normally covered with either stone or slate tiles. Again, the richly decorated hammerbeam roofs are the finest examples.

In areas where timber was plentiful and stone scarce, wattle and daub timber-framed manor houses were built. The interior layout often identical to their stone counterparts.

During the 15th Century large, two-storey bay windows were incorporated into manors. Where they only projected from an upper storey they were called *oriel* windows (originally a term used for a projecting balcony or platform).

Castles (Figures 144 and 145)

Early castles continued on the keep-and-bailey design, although separate great halls with solar,

Figure 144   *Tower of London*

pantry and buttery were often built within the bailey defences. Battlements (notched or indented parapit walls said to be *crenellated*), were incorporated on top of the stone wall surrounding the bailey. Additional defensive towers were added to the bailey wall and sometimes even the keep was incorporated into it. During the 14th Century, these battlements were corbelled out (machicollated) to enable boiling oil and other such unpleasant objects to be dropped on the attackers below. Entrance gates were protected by gatehouses which included drawbridges and a portcullis.

Town houses (Figures 146 and 147)
High encircling walls with defensive towers were built around towns to protect the wealthy merchants who lived within them. Often these surrounded a castle and formed its outer defences.

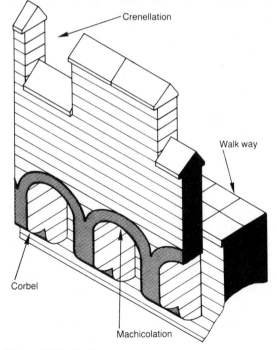

Figure 145   *Battlements*

As land was scarce within the fortified towns, the houses were built very close together. Streets were little more than alley-ways, being usually only 2 to 3 metres wide. These houses were built on a box-frame principle, consisting of beams and vertical posts secured together with carpentry joints and wooden pegs. The upper floors overhung the lower walls for stability, forming jetties. The pans between the posts were filled with wattle and daub. Sometimes *pargetting* (Figure 148) (decorative patterned plasterwork) was used to finish the walls. Windows were glazed with small leaded lights.

Roofs were built with their gables facing the street and finished with decoratively carved barge boards. Roof covering continued to be mainly thatch although stone or slate tiles were used for some buildings.

Many town houses were built for trading purposes with a work shop on the ground floor and family living rooms above.

Rubbish and waste was often thrown into the streets and left to rot. Vermin multiplied, resulting in the bubonic plague or Black Death

Figure 146 *Photograph of a timber-framed town house*

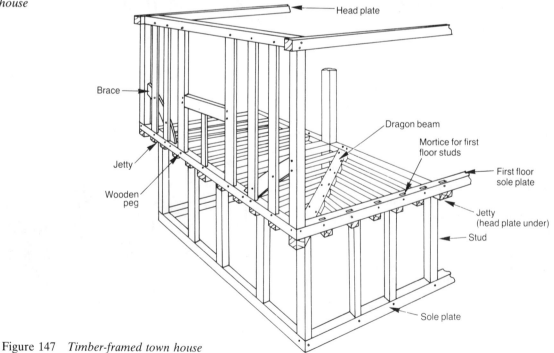

Figure 147 *Timber-framed town house*

during the mid-14th Century, which killed about a third of the population. Many crops were left to rot in the fields as labour was in short supply. In desperation, many land owners turned to sheep farming which required relatively little tending. Land owners soon grew rich on the profits from the booming wool trade. During the perpendicular period, this resulted in a rapid building programme of manor houses, bridges, town halls, market places and inns.

Figure 148　*Pargetting*

Self-assessment questions

Question

1 Define wattle and daub construction

2 State the reason that pit dwellings were built

Your answer

_____

_____

_____

_____

_____

_____

_____

_____

3 With the aid of a sketch, describe the framework of a cruck house

4 Describe the origin of the term 'window pane'

5 Name the collective term for Saxon and Norman architecture

6 Produce a sketch to show the quoins of a Saxon church tower

7 Name and describe the first type of Norman castle

8 State the purpose of a solar in a manor house

9 Name the *three* storeys used to give height within churches

_____
_____
_____
_____

10 Describe a groined vault with the aid of a sketch

11 State the meaning of the term 'Gothic'

_____
_____
_____
_____

12 Illustrate and state the purpose of a flying buttress

13 Sketch a lancet arch window and name the period when they were in common use

_____
_____
_____
_____

14 Which one of the following
features is *not* normally associated with Gothic architecture:
(a) curved window tracery
(b) semi-circular headed doors
(c) groined ribbed vault
(d) pointed, arch-topped win-
    dows?   ⌐ a ⌐   ⌐ b ⌐   ⌐ c ⌐   ⌐ d ⌐

15 Church towers with broach
spires are a feature of which
period:
(a) Norman
(b) Early English
(c) decorated
(d) perpendicular?   ⌐ a ⌐   ⌐ b ⌐   ⌐ c ⌐   ⌐ d ⌐

The history of building – from Tudor to the present day

Table 9 gives the dates and architectural periods from Tudor times onwards. Remember these are simple classifications given to them by historians, and often the styles overlap the periods.

Table 9 **The historical styles of building—II**

Date	Period/style	Title	Features
1485 – 1558	Tudor		Red brick, palaces, timber-box frame, Reformation and dissolution of the monasteries, decorative brick chimneys
1558 – 1603 1603 – 1625 1625 – 1702	Elizabethan Jacobean Stuart	Renaissance	Classical style, numerous large windows, the Civil War, Cromwell's government, restoration of monarchy, Great Fire of London, window tax
1695 – 1725 1720 – 1760 1760 – 1800 1810 – 1837	Baroque Palladian Adam Regency	Georgian (1702 – 1837)	Town planning, squares and terraces of fine houses, sliding sash windows, stucco, brick tax, elaborate interiors
1837 – 1901	Victorian		Battle of the styles, Gothic revival, Crystal Palace, Industrial Revolution, spread of industrial towns, back-to-back housing, cast iron, portland cement, monumental public buildings, electric lighting, telephone, Public Health Act, tap water and outside lavatories become common
1901 – 1910 1910 – onwards	Edwardian Modern	Twentieth century	Introduction of garden cities, first Town Planning Act, two World Wars, jerry-building, ribbon development, new towns, reinforced concrete, steel frame, high-rise construction, system building, council housing, increasing comfort in housing

Tudor

Tudor architecture is seen as the transitional period between **perpendicular Gothic** and the **Renaissance**. In 1485, peace had returned to England with the end of the civil war called the Wars of the Roses. This conflict had lasted some thirty years. Many of the baron's family fortunes had been ruined as a result.

King Henry VIII's matrimonial problems meanwhile caused conflict with the established church. This led to the Reformation and the rise of the Church of England, with the dissolution of the monasteries. Their estates were confiscated and sold to merchants and farmers who would support the king. Thus, many new large farms were established by the gentry, who went on in turn to build smaller farms for their yeoman and cottages for their labourers. At the same time, the king (using the profits from the dissolution) was encouraging the building of palaces and large country mansions.

Palaces and mansions (Figure 149)

Many affluent gentry built themselves large mansions standing in their own private landscaped parks. Typically, these mansions were of two types: earlier they were built around a courtyard or quadrangle with an elaborate gate house; later they consisted of basically a large rectangular building onto which short projecting wings and porches were attached, giving the familiar **E**- or **H**-shaped plan. These mansions contained a great number of private rooms, although the richly decorated and furnished great hall remained the show-piece. Elaborately carved oak staircases gave access to the long gallery on the first floor which ran the length of the house. It was used for exercise, music and conversation. Interior walls were often covered with decorative plain or linenfold oak panelling. (A *linenfold panel* is one that has been carved to resemble a folded piece of linen.) Ceilings began to be plastered (an Italian influence) with ornate decorative relief patterns.

Brick was the prestigious building material for the mansions. At first it was imported from Flanders as balast in the returning wool ships; later brick kilns were set up in eastern England. Sometimes dark-blue diapered patterns were included in the red brick work. These were

Figure 149   *Tudor palace (Hampton Court)*

formed using the bricks that had over-heated in the kiln and turned colour (see Figure 150).

Sometimes gables were extended past the roof line and finished in a step fashion known as *crow steps*, or curved. Mock battlements forming a parapit wall were often included at the roof eaves for decorative purposes. Roofs were tiled in clay or slate, and the rainwater they shed was discharged into decorative lead hopperheads and rainwater pipes (see Figure 151). Chimney stacks of brick were introduced; in fact, they became a marked decorative feature of the times. These tall and ornate chimneys, often like giant corkscrews, were built of necessity in order to extract the noxious fumes given off by coal which had just started to be burnt (see Figure 152).

Figure 152　*Tudor chimney stacks*

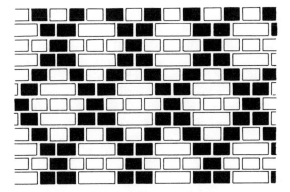

Figure 150　*Diapered-pattern brickwork*

Windows were framed in stone with either a square, flat head or topped by a flattened, four-centred arch. The area of the window was divided up by stone mullions and transoms into which the leaded lights were set. Bay and oriel windows were increasingly used as a design feature.

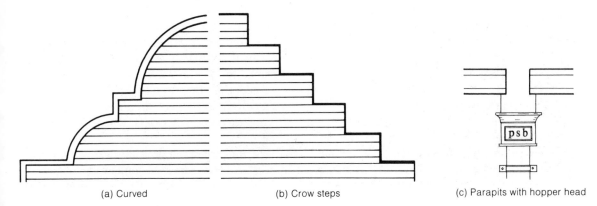

(a) Curved　　　　　　(b) Crow steps　　　　　　(c) Parapits with hopper head

Figure 151　*Gable ends and parapits*

Figure 153   *Tudor-jetted timber-framed house*

Houses (Figure 153)

The majority of small houses were constructed from timber using the box-frame principle, placed on a stone foundation. As timber became more expensive, the space between the posts became wider, and as a result diagonal braces had to be added to ensure rigidity. Later these braces were carved in a variety of shapes and became a distinctive decorative feature. The pans were filled with panels of either lime-washed wattle and daub, or brickwork in decorative patterns.

Fireplaces of brick were built outwards like a little room at the end of a house. Often they contained seats on either side with the fire in the middle, known as an *ingle nook*. These were topped by tall elaborate chimney stacks which are a prominent feature of Tudor timber-frame houses.

Windows were timber casements glazed with leaded lights. Roofs were still weathered in thatch or tiles of clay or slate. Access to the upper floors (which had previously been via a ladder), was now replaced by a short steep staircase. Often this was a spiral to save space. Again interior walls were often covered with plain or linenfold oak panelling. As well as being a decorative finish, the panelling also served to keep out the damp and draughts by covering the holes in the pan infilling.

Renaissance

Up until the end of the Tudor period, people basically built their houses as it pleased them, although most would normally employ a master carpenter and mason for advice on design and building method. By the 17th Century, however, the design and planning of buildings was considered a specialist task. Thus the architect appears on the scene. It was considered important for them to travel to Italy in order to study their buildings which copied the Ancient Greek and Roman Classical styles.

The term 'Renaissance' means the rebirth or rediscovery; thus the Renaissance period sees the rediscovery of Classical style which is based on symmetry and the concept of orders, each part being mathematical in proportion and related to each other.

Each of the orders is an assembly consisting of a base, column, capital, entablature (moulded beam or lintel above a column) and pediment (a triangular gable end). There are five orders: Doric, Ionic, Corinthian, Tuscan and Composite. The first three have both Greek and Roman versions, whilst the Tuscan and the Composite were added by the Romans (see Figure 154).

The Greeks used a column-and-beam method of construction. When the Romans colonized Greece they incorporated the column and beam orders into their arch and dome buildings, although often as merely applied decoration.

By the time of Elizabeth I's accession in 1558 the religious problems of the country had largely been overcome. Also the prosperity of the

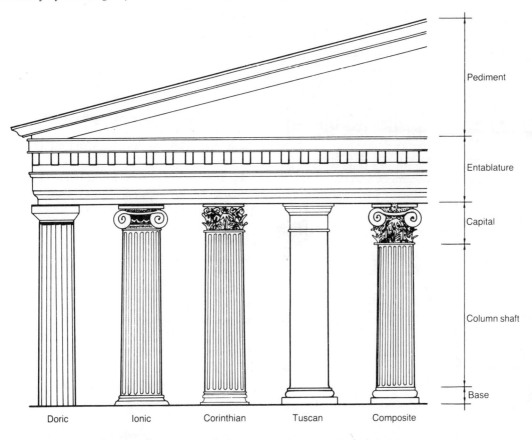

Figure 154   *Architectural orders*

country was just beginning to revive after the near bankruptcy caused by Henry VIII's spendthrift policy.

Mansion houses (Figure 155)

Mansion-house plans continued on the Tudor **E** and **H** shapes and moved towards greater symmetry. Windows continued to use leaded lights set in rectangular stone mullioned and transomed surrounds although they became much larger. Many were said to have 'more glass than wall'. Roof lines were broken with curved and triangular gables, turrets, lanterns and chimneys. Chimneys were now rectangular, made to resemble Classical columns and usually grouped together in two's or three's. The central feature was often a two- or three-storeyed entrance porch with semi-circular headed doors and superimposed Classical orders and topped with a triangular or segmental pediment. By the early 17th Century, architects were beginning to design houses on a rectangular plan.

Inigo Jones (Figure 156)

Inigo Jones, the first important architect in the country was appointed Surveyor General to the Crown in 1615. He brought the true Italian style to England; this is often known as *Palladian* after the Italian architect Palladio. He built the Banqueting Hall in Whitehall and the Queen's House in Greenwich. The exteriors were of a more regular symmetric design, the roof line did not project above the walls, windows and doors were topped with pediments and all the principal rooms were on the first floor.

This style was a complete contrast to anything

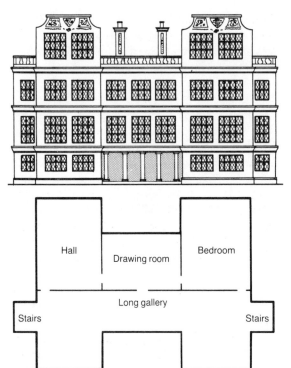

Figure 155 *'H' plan manor house*

seen before, and had a profound influence on architecture for years to come.

Houses

The small houses of the time continued to be mainly timber frame although by the early 17th Century jetties were discontinued as being a fire risk by James I's decree. The timber posts of the frame now were continuous from the ground to the eaves.

In clay areas, brick lower walls (with tile hanging to the upper storey) were popular, whilst in chalk districts 'knapped' flint in a brick framework was common. In parts of the West Country, cob-walled (layers of pressed mud, gravel and straw) and thatch-roofed cottages were popular.

After the Civil War between the Royalists and the Parliamentarians, which culminated with the execution of Charles I in 1649, Oliver Cromwell was made Lord Protector. This had a restraining effect on house design, sweeping away much of the crude over-elaboration. In 1660 with the restoration of the monarchy (Charles II), house

Figure 156 *Inigo Jones (banqueting hall)*

design once again flourished. The Great Plague spread ruthlessly through London in 1665; this was halted only by the Great Fire in 1666 which destroyed over 13,000 buildings.

Sir Christopher Wren (see Figure 157)

Christopher Wren, who was appointed by Charles II in 1661 Assistant to the Surveyor General, planned a new City of London. Although much of his plan was never realized, he was responsible for re-building St. Paul's Cathedral and many other London churches. He introduced Portland stone to London for church and town-house building. Wren successfully combined the Palladian style with such English features as steeply-pitched roofs, large windows and chimney stacks. His designs became the foundation for the Georgian houses of the next century. He used the recently invented vertical-sliding sash window, pediments above the main entrance doors, and pitched roofs with hipped ends and dormer windows. For smaller domestic houses he pioneered a style which later became known as *Queen Anne style*. Exteriors were symmetrical, and of plain brick with

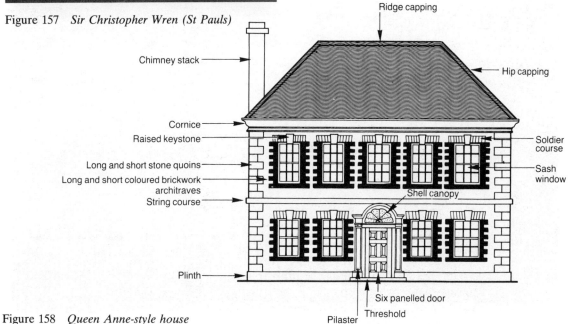

Figure 158 *Queen Anne-style house*

projecting stone quoins. Windows were framed by architraves of long and short raised or coloured brickwork often with a decorated key stone (see Figure 158).

Taxes

In 1661 a Chimney Tax of 2 shillings (10 p) was levied for every chimney. The poorest homes did without, letting the fumes drift out through a smoke-hole in the roof. Fortunately, this was soon repealed.

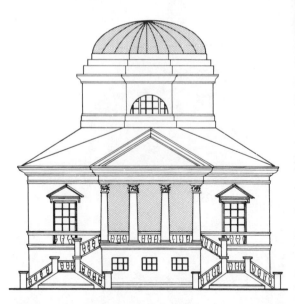

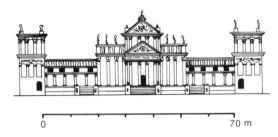
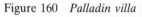

Figure 159   *English baroque*

Figure 160   *Palladin villa*

Figure 161   *Robert Adam (Fitzroy Square)*

Figure 162   *Adam's fanlight*

A window tax was introduced in 1697 and survived right up until 1851. This was levied on houses with more than six glass windows. As a result, many existing windows were often bricked in to avoid paying this annual tax of: 2 shillings (10 p) for up to 9 windows; 6 shillings (30 p) for up to 19 windows; 10 shillings (50 p) for 20 or more.

Georgian

Baroque

This period is often called the Age of Elegance. During the early part of this era some very grand, highly-decorative, extravagant houses were built, in a Classical style known as *English Baroque*. Sir John Vanbrugh was the leading architect of this style, Blenheim Palace being the major example, as illustrated by Figure 159.

Palladianism (Figure 160)

After about 25 years of the very expensive Baroque style, architecture returned to the more sober classical styles of *Palladianism*. During this period, because of the density of houses in towns some thought was given to *town planning*. Instead of single detached houses, architects designed terraced houses in whole streets, squares and crescents. By treating them as a whole, what were comparatively small houses were given the style and dignity of a palace. At the forefront of this town-planning movement were architects John Wood & Son who were responsible for developing large areas of Bath.

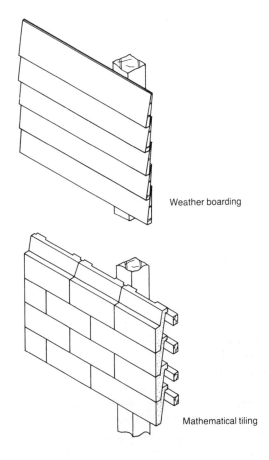

Weather boarding

Mathematical tiling

Figure 163   *Alternatives to bricks*

Figure 164   *Regency (Regents Park Crescent)*

Robert Adam (Figure 161)

Robert Adam, one of the great architects of the 18th Century, further developed Georgian town planning and laid out much of London. In addition to designing the buildings, he planned every detail of their interior, including their fireplaces and sometimes even furniture, although the big names in furniture at the time were Sheraton, Chippendale and Hepplewhite.

Adam's doorways had semi-circular fanlights over them with glazing bars of cast iron resembling a spider's web. Balconies were made of iron, and iron railings in front of terraces were popular (see Figure 162). Stucco was brought to England from Scotland by Adam. This was a fine plaster applied at first only to the ground-floor brickwork, into which lines were pressed to imitate stone jointing. Roof pitches were lower; frequently the slated slope was concealed by parapit wall and cornices raised above the eaves.

Internally, Adam used curved walls and alcoves, ceilings and pilasters (half columns placed against a wall). All were elaborated in fine moulded plaster which was painted and guilded. Other striking internal features are the elegant white marble fireplaces and the ceilings painted with patterns and fine pictures by artists brought across from Italy. Many of these town houses had stabling accommodation in the rear garden (including that for coachmen); access to this was via a rear mews.

Workers' housing (Figure 163)

Outside the main towns, semi-detached and terraced cottages were being built by some wealthy land owners for their workers. These were either of total brick, timber-frame covered in horizontal weatherboards or a combination of the two, with a brick lower storey and a weatherboard upper one. Tile hanging and pargetting were still popular in certain areas, as was *mathematical tiling* (a tile that resembled brickwork). These alternatives to brickwork were brought in mainly after 1784 when the and Regent's Park, Marble Arch and the Brighton Royal Pavillion. Nash favoured the use of stucco to cover the whole of a building and not just the lower storey as Adam had done. It was fashionable at this time for wealthy people to live in seaside or spa towns (health centres where it was possible to bathe in the local water) for part of the year. There are mainly Regency terraces in towns such as Bath, Brighton, Cheltenham, Hove, Hastings and Leamington. Often a striking feature of these terraces is their curved fronts, bay and bow windows and balconies topped with curved metal canopies.

Shops of the time were still often an extension of the home. Typically, they consisted of a central doorway flanked on either side by bow windows, used for display purposes, as shown in Figure 166.

Victorian

The Victorians were prolific builders. This was out of necessity as the population had risen from 8.9 million in 1801 (first official census in England and Wales) to 32.5 million in 1901. This was attributed to a higher birth rate, and a fall in death rate owing to increased standards of hygiene and medical care. In fact, more buildings were constructed in this period, than in all the previous periods put together, right back to the prehistoric ages.

Figure 165   *Regency canopy and wrought iron work*

brick tax was introduced, forcing builders to avoid bricks as far as possible. This tax, which was not repealed until 1850, rose from 2 shillings and six pence (12½ p) per thousand bricks in 1784 to 10 shillings (50 p) per thousand by 1803.

Regency (Figures 164 and 165)

This is the last stage of the Georgian period when George, Prince of Wales, was Regent during the last years of his father's (George II) reign.

Adam's influence continued in town planning and house building in the Georgian style. John Nash is the architect most often associated with the Regency. Among his most famous buildings are Buckingham Palace, works in Regent Street

Industrial revolution

The Industrial Revolution which had started in the 18th Century was accelerating rapidly, and large numbers of the population were moving from the country to the industrial areas. This created new centres of populations. In order to provide facilities for industry and this expanding population, a tremendous, but largely unplanned, uncontrolled, building drive was put in operation. An extensive railway system, a canal and road network, factories, offices, shops, houses, and educational, public and civic buildings were all developed.

During the early **Victorian period** there was the so-called *battle of the styles* taking place,

Figure 166   *Bow front shops*

where the Classical style was being used for most civic and public buildings, whilst churches and houses were seeing a revival of Gothic architecture. This *Gothic revival movement* continued to grow and by the mid-19th Century many town halls, educational buildings and stations, etc., were built using this style (Houses of Parliament, St. Pancras Station, Tower Bridge) (see Figures 167 and 168).

During this period, engineering came to the fore. Engineers explored the possibilities of sheet glass, cast iron and steel, which were now available in large quantities as a result of mass production. They built massive glasshouses (Palm House at Kew Gardens), exhibition halls (Crystal Palace), factories and railway stations out of standard iron girders, stanchions and sheets of glass, prefabricated in a factory and assembled on-site. Iron and steel also made possible the many wide-spanning canal and

railway bridges. Industrial buildings were normally constructed as purely functional, little attention being paid to their aesthetic appearance.

Houses (Figures 169, 170 and 171)

The well-off people of the time inhabited the outer suburbs of an area, where there was space, trees and fresh air. Most of the suburban housing was detached or semi-detached, built in Gothic revival, when every type of unnecessary tower, pinnacle, spire, turret, battlement, decorative brickwork, stained-glass leaded lights and diapering were added to the outside of a house as a status symbol. The interiors of the houses matched their exteriors, where everything was considered fussy, ornate and colourful.

Later, the typical Victorian person's house became a terraced two or three storey, often

Figure 167 *Victorian gothic revival (Houses of Parliament)*

Figure 168 *Victorian gothic revival (Tower Bridge)*

Figure 169   *Victorian detached villa*

with a basement. Other characteristics included: slate roof with crested ridge tiles; sash windows in bays with decorated pillars and lintels; stained leaded light glass in entrance door and fanlight; decorative half-tiled recessed entrance porch; tiled front path; fireplace in every room and an outside toilet but with an inside cold-water tap.

⚹Factory workers' homes were often back-to-back houses, terraced on three sides (having windows only at the front) or lines of terraces built close together. Only a narrow street ran between them at the front and a small yard, and alley-way wide enough for the night-soil man's horse and cart at the rear.⚹The inhabitants of these houses would share a communal water tap and earth toilet, which would be emptied by the

night-soil man, may be monthly. These drab functional buildings had little thought given to design and were soon labelled as *slums.*⚹

Other workers were housed in blocks of flats mostly converted from Georgian terraces. With their large number of occupants, they too quickly became slum areas.

Housing improvements (Figure 172)

Some wealthy businessmen and landowners built model dwellings. For example, George Peabody, an American merchant, financed the building of tenement blocks to house the poor. Towards the end of the century whole communities including schools, shops and churches were being built by some businessmen to provide better living standards for their workforce. Sir Titus Salt built Saltaire in 1871; the Lever Brothers built Port Sunlight in 1886; Cadbury's built Bourneville in 1895; and finally Sir Joseph Rowntree built Earswick in 1905.

The Public Health Act of 1875 did much to improve the standards of water supply and sewage disposal. This Act also covered the collection of household refuse and street cleaning.

In 1890 the Government passed an Act which provided loans to local authorities for house building and made the clearance of back-to-back slums a priority.

By the turn of the 19th Century, electric lighting had been introduced into towns, and most houses had a cold water tap and an outside toilet. Bathrooms were still rare, most people still taking their bath in metal tubs placed in front of a fire or range.

The twentieth century

Styles did not suddenly change with the commencement of the Edwardian era in 1901. In the early years, architects followed the Victorian fashion of favouring the Gothic revival mainly for churches and using the Classical styles for civic and commercial buildings. By now, however, the structural steel frame had been largely adopted for the superstructure, with the Gothic

Figure 170   *Victorian terraced house*

or Classical façades (exterior faces of a building) simply becoming a non-load-bearing external envelope.

Garden cities (Figures 173 and 174)

In 1902, Ebenezer Howard published a book called *Garden Cities of Tomorrow*. He suggested that it was wrong for workers to be housed in cramped unhealthy inner-city areas. Instead, medium-size communities of about 32,000 people should be built, each complete with their own facilities, industries and planned layout surrounded by countryside (green belt).

This led to the building of Letchworth in 1903, 'the first garden city', and Welwyn in 1920. Houses, each with their own garden, were grouped in tree-lined, grass-verged crescents,

Figure 171   *Victorian terraced factory workers' houses*

Figure 172   *Peabody Trust tenements (Victoria)*

development). Unfortunately, the boom encouraged speculators into house building, with little building knowledge. These people who used shoddy material and short-cut methods to secure a quick profit gave rise to the terms 'jerry-building', 'jerry-built' and 'jerry-builders', etc.

By the start of the Second World War in 1939 the typical house, having front and rear gardens, was of brick construction often pebble-dashed. Windows were casements with bays at the front and French windows at the rear. Most had gas and electricity connected for cooking and lighting, although coal and coke were used for heating. The interior consisted of three bed-

Figure 173   *Letchworth Garden City*

closes and small side roads, thus avoiding the long monotonous rows of buildings. This ideal was later copied to various extents throughout the country. The influence of garden cities can be seen in almost every New Town and housing estate built since.

Between the Wars (Figure 175)
Building programmes were stopped in 1914 with the outbreak of the First World War, causing a severe housing shortage by the end of the War in 1918. During the subsequent housing boom, local authorities built houses to rent and private developers built ones for sale. Much of this was endless rows of semi-detached and terraced housing lining the roads linking towns (*ribbon*

Figure 174   *Typical garden city avenue*

Figure 175   *Between the wars semi's*

Figure 176   *Modern architecture (Milton Keynes)*

Figure 177   *Typical new town view (Letchworth)*

Figure 178   *High-rise estate*

Figure 179   *Plain modern house*

rooms, a lounge, dining room, kitchen, bath-room and toilet. *Bungalows* also had a sudden rise to popularity at this time.

Prefabs

Again, during the War years building was at a standstill. Even after the end of the Second World War in 1945, very little building was carried out, as materials were in short supply and a licence to build was required. With a shortage of one million homes, a *prefabricated house-building programme* was started by the Government. These 'prefabs' were factory-made in sections from aluminium, concrete or steel and then transported to site for erection. They were fairly small and built close together, although each had its own little garden.

In spite of the fact that prefabs were a stop-gap measure having a life-span of up to ten years, some were homes for more than twenty-five years. With their advantages of massed-produced factory construction in controlled conditions, and speed of erection, prefabs

Figure 180   *Neo-Georgian modern house*

became the forerunner of the later system-building boom, which used prefabricated components of concrete, steel or timber.

Modern architecture (Figure 176)

This had its roots with architects such as Frank Lloyd Wright and Le Corbusier. Modern architectural style is based on *functionalism*. Its shape is not preconceived but evolves after a careful study of its occupants' needs. Typically, modern buildings have become simple rectangles with large windows or transparent walls and open-plan interiors. Exteriors are without ornaments or decoration but not plain; instead the modern architecture uses contrasting colours and textures to create effect.

New Towns (Figure 177)

The 1946 New Towns Act and the 1947 Town and Country Planning Act were introduced to ease the housing shortage and prevent a return to the jerry-building and ribbon development of the post-War years.

The New Towns Act enabled the establishment of New Towns by Development Corporations financed by the Government. Harlow, Stevenage, Crawley, Corby, Cumbernauld and Milton Keynes are some examples. They are built as complete residential/industrial units on the garden-city principle, although much larger. Most are examples of mixed developments with all kinds of houses, flats, maisonettes for families, couples and singles, and also single-storey buildings for the elderly and handicapped. At the same time, planned expansions of existing towns and cities were taking place in the form of new housing estates. Some like the New Towns were mixed developments.

Figure 181   *Mock Tudor modern house*

High rise (Figure 178)

High-rise blocks of flats were used in inner-city areas to replace bombed-out sites and to re-develop slum areas. These are often considered unpopular, both socially and economically. This is because of problems, firstly associated with their density, e.g. noise, loss of privacy, mental stress and vandalism, and secondly, because of their high maintenance cost often caused through poor design, poor construction or vandalism.

Today's houses

Whatever their external appearances, today's houses are full of home comforts and labour-saving devices. Electric irons, vacuum cleaners, radios, televisions, hi-fi, washing machines and refrigerators were becoming increasingly used during the 1950s. Oil, gas, or electric central heating was widely installed by the 1970s. Dishwashers, tumble dryers, microwave ovens, videos and microcomputers were introduced during the 1970s and 1980s. Garaging and off-street parking were increasingly provided for from the late 1950s onwards. Windows got much larger during the 1960s with the advent of cheap *float glass*, although in the 1980s they got smaller again or were double glazed because of thermal-insulation controls. Increasingly, since the 1970s, standards of thermal insulation have improved because of the pending shortage and escalating cost of energy.

It would be inappropriate to describe the external features of a present-day house as has been done for the previous periods: there is no one predominant style. They range from plain modern and pedimented 'Neo-Georgian' right through to applied beam 'Mock-Tudor', as shown by Figures 179–181.

Self-assessment questions

Question	*Your answer*

1 State the meaning of the term 'Renaissance'

_____

_____

_____

_____

2 Distinguish between Greek and Roman forms of Classical architecture

_____

_____

_____

_____

3 An architect by the name of Nash often used stucco to cover the façades of his buildings
  (i) describe what stucco is; and
  (ii) name the period when it was popular

_____

_____

_____

_____

4 Describe, with the aid of a sketch, 'mathematical tiling'

5 Name the building styles and architectural period that are associated with the 'battle of styles'

_____

_____

_____

_____

6 Describe the type of house occupied by a typical early Victorian factory worker

_____

_____

_____

_____

7 Define the following terms:
  (i) ribbon development
  (ii) jerry-building

_____

_____

_____

_____

8 Describe the features of modern architectural style

_____

_____

_____

_____

9 State the reason that prefabs were introduced after 1945

_____

_____

_____

_____

10 Produce an outline sketch to illustrate the features of a Queen Anne style house

11 Describe, with the aid of a sketch, diapered patterned brickwork

12 Produce a sketch to show the difference between Ionic and Tuscan architectural orders

13 Describe the main feature of
   the Bath terraces, built by
   Woods & Son

   _____

   _____

   _____

   _____

14 Corkscrew chimney stacks
   are a feature of which style?
   (a) Victorian
   (b) Adam
   (c) Regency
   (d) Tudor?   ⌐ a ⌐   ⌐ b ⌐   ⌐ c ⌐   ⌐ d ⌐

15 Ebenezer Howard was the
   pioneer of:
   (a) New towns
   (b) garden cities
   (c) workers' tenements
   (d) modern architecture?   ⌐ a ⌐   ⌐ b ⌐   ⌐ c ⌐   ⌐ d ⌐

Assignment three

Approximately three hours are required to answer this assignment

Assignments are intended to illustrate some of the day-to-day problems/enquiries which you as a member of the building industry may encounter.

For the purposes of this assignment you are to assume that you have recently completed your apprenticeship/training period and have now been promoted to an assistant foreman. Your company employs a small work force of highly skilled craft operatives and specializes in the restoration of period buildings.

You should attempt all six tasks of this assignment. Illustrate your answers with sketches where appropriate.

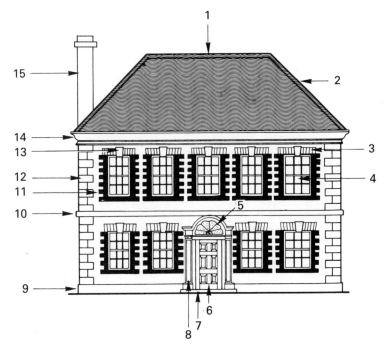

Figure 182   *Front elevation*

Task one

You are currently employed on the restoration of the period building illustrated in Figure 182.

1 Name the type/period of the building

2 To ensure that the terminology in the specification is readily understood by everyone, indicate on Figure 182 the names of the numbered features/components

Task two

3 In addition to the refurbishment, it is proposed to erect a new garage/workshop at the rear of the plot indicated in the site plan, Figure 183.
Produce sketch designs for this new building, which blends sympathetically with the existing house

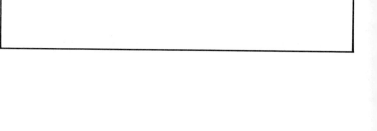

Task three

4 Prepare a list of materials for the new garage/workshop

Task four

5 Name and briefly describe the purpose of any statutory controls which may effect the (i) restoration; and (ii) new garage/workshop

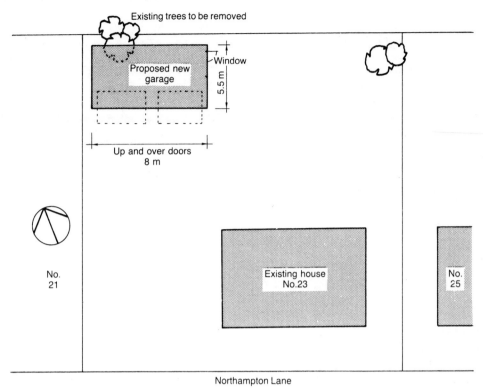

Existing trees to be removed

Proposed new garage

Window

5.5 m

Up and over doors
8 m

No.
21

Existing house
No.23

No.
25

Northampton Lane

Figure 183   *Site plan*

Task five

6 Your company also acts in an advisory capacity to a local open-air cultural museum. Forming the major part of their exhibits are a number of reconstructed period buildings. Produce a sketch for use by the unskilled volunteer erectors to show the position of the dragon beam to a jetted timber frame house

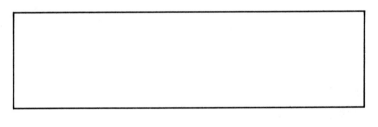

Task six

7 You have been asked by the
museum management to assist
them in the preparation of
information cards. Write a
brief description suitable for
displaying alongside the following exhibits: (i) a bullion
pane of crown glass; (ii) a
mathematical tile; (iii) a section of pargetting

Index